D1481937

The Oklahoma City Bombing

Tamara L. Roleff, *Book Editor*

Daniel Leone, *President*
Bonnie Szumski, *Publisher*
Scott Barbour, *Managing Editor*
David M. Haugen, *Series Editor*

GREENHAVEN
PRESS ®

THOMSON

GALE

San Diego • Detroit • New York • San Francisco • Cleveland
New Haven, Conn. • Waterville, Maine • London • Munich

LIBRARY OF CONGRESS CATALOGING-IN-PUBLICATION DATA

The Oklahoma City bombing / Tamara L. Roleff, book editor.
    p. cm. — (History firsthand)
Includes bibliographical references and index.
ISBN 0-7377-1659-2 (pbk. : alk. paper) — ISBN 0-7377-1658-4 (lib. : alk. paper)
    1. Oklahoma City Federal Building Bombing, Oklahoma City, Okla., 1995.
2. Terrorism—Oklahoma—Oklahoma City. 3. Victims of terrorism—Oklahoma—Oklahoma City—Case studies. 4. Rescue work—Oklahoma—Oklahoma City—Case studies. 5. McVeigh, Timothy. I. Roleff, Tamara L., 1959– . II. Series.
HV6432.6.O35 2004
976.6'38.053—dc21
                                         2003055105

Contents

Chapter 4: Understanding Timothy McVeigh

Chapter 5: The Trial and Execution

court that McVeigh told him about his plot to blow up
the federal building in Oklahoma City.

Chapter 6: The Memorial

Foreword

In his preface to a book on the events leading to the Civil War, Stephen B. Oates, the historian and biographer of Abraham Lincoln, John Brown, and other noteworthy American historical figures, explained the difficulty of writing history in the traditional third-person voice of the biographer and historian. "The trouble, I realized, was the detached third-person voice," wrote Oates. "It seemed to wring all the life out of my characters and the antebellum era." Indeed, how can a historian, even one as prominent as Oates, compete with the eloquent voices of Daniel Webster, Abraham Lincoln, Harriet Beecher Stowe, Frederick Douglass, and Robert E. Lee?

Oates's comment notwithstanding, every student of history, professional and amateur alike, can name a score of excellent accounts written in the traditional third-person voice of the historian that bring to life an event or an era and the people who lived through it. In *Battle Cry of Freedom*, James M. McPherson vividly re-creates the American Civil War. Barbara Tuchman's *The Guns of August* captures in sharp detail the tensions in Europe that led to the outbreak of World War I. Taylor Branch's *Parting the Waters* provides a detailed and dramatic account of the American Civil Rights Movement. The study of history would be impossible without such guiding texts.

Nonetheless, Oates's comment makes a compelling point. Often the most convincing tellers of history are those who lived through the event, the eyewitnesses who recorded their firsthand experiences in autobiographies, speeches, memoirs, journals, and letters. The Greenhaven Press History Firsthand series presents history through the words of first-person narrators. Each text in this series captures a significant historical era or event—the American Civil War, the

Great Depression, the Holocaust, the Roaring Twenties, the 1960s, the Vietnam War. Readers will investigate these historical eras and events by examining primary-source documents, authored by chroniclers both famous and little known. The texts in the History Firsthand series comprise the celebrated and familiar words of the presidents, generals, and famous men and women of letters who recorded their impressions for posterity, as well as the statements of the ordinary people who struggled to understand the storm of events around them—the foot soldiers who fought the great battles and their loved ones back home, the men and women who waited on the breadlines, the college students who marched in protest.

The texts in this series are particularly suited to students beginning serious historical study. By examining these firsthand documents, novice historians can begin to form their own insights and conclusions about the historical era or event under investigation. To aid the student in that process, the texts in the History Firsthand series include introductions that provide an overview of the era or event, timelines, and bibliographies that point the serious student toward key historical works for further study.

The study of history commences with an examination of words—the testimony of witnesses who lived through an era or event and left for future generations the task of making sense of their accounts. The Greenhaven Press History Firsthand series invites the beginner historian to commence the process of historical investigation by focusing on the words of those individuals who made history by living through it and recording their experiences firsthand.

Introduction

S hortly before 9 A.M. on Wednesday, April 19, 1995, a man driving a Ryder truck parked in front of the Alfred P. Murrah Federal Building in downtown Oklahoma City. At least one man (some witnesses claim they saw two men) got out of the truck and walked quickly away. A few minutes later a huge explosion shook the entire downtown area, shattering windows in buildings blocks away. The explosion was heard and felt for miles. The downtown area had been having problems with gas leaks, and at first, many people thought a gas line had ruptured and exploded. But when they saw that the federal building had been totally destroyed, they realized that a bomb was responsible for the destruction.

Almost immediately, bystanders began running to the building to help in any way they could. Parents came looking for their children who had been left in the day-care center on the federal building's second floor. Husbands and wives searched the crowd for their spouses. Hospitals sent medical teams to the site to help the injured, and called in off-duty doctors, nurses, and paramedics to treat the hundreds of wounded they expected to receive. But as the day wore on, it soon became clear that although there were plenty of injured people to treat, body bags would be needed more than medical workers. The last survivor was pulled from the rubble at about 10 P.M. that night, although rescuers continued to search for survivors—and then for bodies—for sixteen more days. All told, 168 people, including 19 children, were killed in the bombing.

An Arrest in Perry, Oklahoma

Roughly an hour and a half after the explosion, Oklahoma state trooper Charles J. Hanger pulled over the driver of a yellow Mercury Marquis because the car did not have a license plate. When Hanger got out of his patrol car, the driver of the Mercury stepped out of his. Hanger instantly went on alert; most people remain in their cars when stopped by a trooper, and Hanger did not like the fact that this driver got out of his car. The driver pulled out his wallet and gave the trooper a driver's license issued to Timothy McVeigh in Michigan. Then Hanger noticed a bulge under the driver's jacket. The trooper pulled out his own gun and pointed it at McVeigh's head as he removed the gun from the driver's shoulder holster, threw it and the ammunition onto the ground, and handcuffed the man. When Hanger asked the man why he was carrying a gun, McVeigh replied that he believed he had every right to do so. Hanger placed McVeigh in the backseat of the patrol car and searched the Mercury. He found a sign that read "Do Not Tow" and a sealed, white, legal-size envelope. When Hanger asked McVeigh if he wanted the envelope, McVeigh told him to just leave it in the car. The car was locked and left on the shoulder of the freeway until McVeigh could make bail and retrieve it.

Hanger brought McVeigh to the county jail in Perry, where he was charged with four misdemeanors: failure to display a license plate, failure to carry proof of insurance, unlawfully carrying a weapon, and transporting a loaded weapon in a motor vehicle. McVeigh waited in jail for two days before he was brought into court for his arraignment. But instead of being released on bail, McVeigh was arrested by the Federal Bureau of Investigation (FBI) on April 21, 1995, for bombing the federal building in Oklahoma City.

The Search Begins

The first break for the FBI had come just a few hours after the bombing. Law enforcement authorities found the rear axle from the Ryder truck a block away from the Murrah building. The FBI found the vehicle identification number on the axle and traced the truck to a rental agency in Junction City, Kansas. According to Eldon Elliott, the owner of the rental agency, he had rented the truck to a man named Robert Kling on Monday, April 17. By 5 P.M. on the day of the bombing, an FBI artist was in Junction City drawing sketches of Robert Kling and the man who had accompanied him to the rental agency.

The day after the bombing, FBI agents took the sketches of Robert Kling, known as John Doe Number 1, and his accomplice, John Doe Number 2, to businesses in Junction City. The manager at the Dreamland Motel, Lea McGowan, recognized John Doe Number 1 as a guest who had stayed for four nights the previous week. But the guest had registered under the name Timothy McVeigh and had given a Michigan address on his registration card. The FBI went to the address in Michigan and discovered it belonged to a farmer named James Nichols. His brother Terry had lived on the farm for a while and so had one of Terry's old army friends, Tim McVeigh.

Meanwhile, FBI agents checked with the National Crime Information Center in Washington, D.C., and discovered that an Oklahoma state trooper had run McVeigh's name through the system at about 10:30 A.M. on April 19 near the town of Perry, Oklahoma. An agent called the sheriff in Perry on Friday morning, April 21, and asked if he still had a man named Timothy McVeigh in jail. A check showed that McVeigh was due in court any minute for his arraignment on the weapons and traffic charges. The agent was ecstatic; he told the sheriff, "Put a hold on him! Don't let him go!"[1] Within minutes FBI agents were in a helicopter on their way to Perry to talk to the main suspect in the Oklahoma City bombing.

Timothy McVeigh

After graduating from high school in 1986, Timothy McVeigh was restless. He had dropped out of business school and worked at a couple of jobs, including one as an armed security officer. Tired of fielding his neighbors' complaints about shooting weapons on his own property, McVeigh decided in 1988 to join an organization that not only allowed its employees to shoot but also encouraged them to do so—the U.S. Army. McVeigh wanted to become an infantryman and hoped to eventually join either the army's Special Forces unit or the Rangers.

McVeigh went through boot camp at Fort Benning, Georgia, where he met two men who would become integral parts of his future—Terry Nichols and Michael Fortier. Nichols and McVeigh became close friends during boot camp despite the difference in their ages. (Nichols, thirty-three, was the oldest recruit in the company.) Many of the soldiers in McVeigh's company thought the friendship between McVeigh and Fortier was strange. McVeigh did not drink or use drugs and he was enthusiastic about army life. Fortier did not share McVeigh's zeal for the army, and he smoked marijuana and abused other drugs on a regular—and frequent—basis. Yet they shared similar political beliefs and enjoyed target shooting, so they got along together well.

McVeigh urged Nichols and Fortier—along with many other soldiers in his unit—to read *The Turner Diaries*, a novel that uses diary entries to describe a citizens' revolution against the government. Earl Turner, a low-level resistance fighter in "the Organization," recounts the history of the uprising, from the beginning when the government instituted harsher gun control laws, to the Organization's attempts to fight back by making a truck bomb to destroy the FBI headquarters in Washington, D.C., and eventually deploying a nuclear bomb against the Pentagon. McVeigh believed that *The Turner Diaries* described many of the problems facing the United States, the chief one being that Americans were allowing the federal government to usurp many of their gun rights.

McVeigh Excels in the Army

In the spring of 1989 Nichols received a hardship discharge and returned to his family in Michigan. Shortly after Nichols left the army, McVeigh was assigned a new job: He became a gunner in a Bradley fighting vehicle, a tanklike troop carrier. He learned to fire wire-guided missiles, machine guns, and a 25-mm cannon. McVeigh was in his element. During live-fire competitions, McVeigh was consistently the top-scoring gunner. He once scored 998 points out of a possible

1,000; later, he earned a perfect score. When military and political officials came to the base for demonstrations, McVeigh was the gunner who was chosen to show the Bradley's fighting potential.

Happy with his job and recognition, McVeigh reenlisted in the army in 1990. He was then asked to try out for the U.S. Army's Special Forces unit, which had been his goal all along. However, before he had the chance to try out, his unit was sent to the Persian Gulf to participate in Operation Desert Storm, the first Gulf War. Despite the tedium, boredom, and stress he experienced during wartime, McVeigh continued to excel in his duties in the Persian Gulf. He received the U.S. Army Commendation Medal for using his Bradley's 25-mm cannon to destroy "an enemy machine-gun emplacement, killing two Iraqi soldiers and forcing the surrender of thirty others from dug-in positions."[2] McVeigh, however, had mixed feelings about the war and his participation in it. He was thrilled to use his weapons skills in real-life situations, but he was not sure war against Iraq and Saddam Hussein was warranted since the United States had not been attacked. In addition, he was upset about being part of a coalition force led by the United Nations to subdue a foreign nation—a "New World Order" scenario that many gun-rights supporters fear will signal the beginning of a war led by the U.S. government against those who are only defending their constitutional right.

Just as the Gulf War was winding down, McVeigh was given the opportunity to try out for the Special Forces. However, after spending several months in the Middle East, where he alternated between just trying to stay alive and trying to stave off boredom, McVeigh was no longer as physically fit or as emotionally prepared to meet the unit's demanding and rigorous requirements. He dropped out of the Special Forces try-out during the first week of the physical evaluation program.

When McVeigh returned to his unit at Fort Riley, his army friends could see that he had changed. Although he continued to be an excellent gunner for the Bradley vehicle, he was no longer as enthusiastic about army life as he had been. When McVeigh received an offer to be the personal door gunner for the battalion commander—a big honor—he turned it down. He then told his surprised commanding officer that he had decided to leave the army. By the end of 1991 McVeigh had returned to his family home in western New York State. For the next year McVeigh worked again as a security guard and traveled the gun-show circuit, buying and selling ammunition and small explosives.

The Siege at Ruby Ridge

In the late summer of 1992 McVeigh was captivated by events unfolding in Ruby Ridge, Idaho. Randy Weaver, a survivalist who lived in an isolated cabin with his wife and four children, had been approached in 1989 by an undercover agent with the Bureau of Alcohol, Tobacco, and Firearms (ATF) who wanted to buy a sawed-off shotgun. Weaver rebuffed the agent's request numerous times before finally giving in and selling him a shotgun that was just slightly shorter than what was allowed by law. The bureau then tried to recruit Weaver to be an informer against a white supremacist group whose headquarters were nearby in exchange for dropping the gun charge. When Weaver refused, a federal grand jury issued an indictment. When Weaver did not appear in court (the letter informing him of the court date gave the wrong date), a warrant was issued for his arrest.

For the next year and a half, the Weavers never left their property. Whenever they left their cabin, everyone—children and adults—always carried a loaded gun. Federal agents kept close surveillance on Weaver, his family, and the twenty acres surrounding his small cabin by using high-powered cameras and overhead reconnaissance flights. On August 21, 1992, six armed federal agents dressed in camouflage attempted to make a physical survey of the Weaver property, but they were detected by the Weavers' dog. The dog's barking brought Weaver, his son Sammy, and a friend named Kevin Harris out of the cabin; all were armed. The Weavers and Harris began looking for whatever had disturbed the dog, and they discovered U.S. marshals nearby. Accounts differ on who fired the first shot, but in the ensuing gun battle, the dog, Sammy, and U.S. marshal William F. Degan were killed.

The remaining marshals called for help, and by the next morning, law enforcement officials from the FBI, ATF, state and local police, county sheriff, National Guard, U.S. Border Patrol, and U.S. Marshal Service had all converged on the mountain where the Weavers had their cabin. The FBI secretly changed its standard rules of engagement. Agents were now allowed to shoot to kill any of the Weavers if they were armed; normally, the rules of engagement permit law enforcement officials to shoot only if threatened by a suspect.

In the early evening of August 22, Randy Weaver; his wife, Vicki, carrying her ten-month-old daughter; and Harris—who were all armed—left the cabin to go to a nearby shed where they had placed Sammy's body until they could bury him. As they were walking to the shed, a sniper shot at Randy Weaver, hitting him in the arm. The group turned and ran back to the cabin. As Vicki Weaver stood inside the cabin, holding the door open for her husband and Harris with one hand and cradling her daughter with the other, the sniper shot again. The bullet hit Vicki Weaver in the head, passed through her, and struck Harris in the arm and chest.

An FBI negotiator tried to convince Weaver and Harris to surrender. On August 30 Weaver finally allowed the negotiator to remove Vicki Weaver's body from the cabin. The negotiator also convinced Harris to leave because he desperately needed medical attention for his gunshot wounds. Weaver finally surrendered the next day, August 31. The men were charged and tried on federal charges of murder, conspiracy, and weapons violations, but a jury acquitted them. Weaver was convicted on two counts: failing to appear in court (for his original court appearance) and violating his bail conditions.

McVeigh was convinced that the siege on Ruby Ridge was evidence that the United States was turning into a police state that was intent on persecuting innocent Americans.

Many other Americans shared his rage over the tactics law enforcement agencies were using to disarm the American people. According to McVeigh, the siege at Ruby Ridge was just the latest example of the government's overzealous attempts to weaken and eventually take away an American citizen's right to bear arms.

The Conflagration in Waco

A few months after the siege at Ruby Ridge, another attempt by federal agents to seize illegal weapons owned by a religious group known as the Branch Davidians led to a fifty-one-day siege in Waco, Texas. On February 28, 1993, seventy-six ATF agents arrived at Mount Carmel, the Davidians' compound outside Waco, to arrest the sect's leader, David Koresh, on charges of illegal possession of weapons and explosives. As at Ruby Ridge, a gun battle erupted, with conflicting accounts of who fired the first shot. Four ATF agents were killed and sixteen were wounded in the shootout; inside the Branch Davidian compound, six Davidians were killed and an unknown number were injured. The FBI soon arrived at the compound and took command of the negotiations to end the standoff.

The next day, ten children were sent out of the compound. The FBI then surrounded the compound with armored vehicles and cut the phone line. Negotiations continued with few results. McVeigh closely monitored the developments at Waco. The attempted raid and subsequent standoff made McVeigh so angry that he felt he had to go to Waco to show his support for the Branch Davidians. At the end of March, he drove to Texas with a supply of pamphlets and bumper stickers to sell. The slogans on the bumper stickers made no secret of his feelings toward the government or its position on gun control: "Fear the Government That Fears Your Gun," "Politicians Love Gun Control," "A Man with a Gun Is a Citizen, a Man Without a Gun Is a Subject," and "When Guns Are Outlawed, I Will Become an Outlaw."

During the few days that McVeigh spent in Waco, he gave an interview to a student journalist from Southern Methodist

University, Michelle Rauch. He told Rauch that the only reason the ATF was in Waco was because "it seems the ATF just wants a chance to play with their toys, paid for by government money."[3] In McVeigh's opinion, federal agents had no right to be serving the arrest warrant in Waco; the local sheriff's office should have been the agency that executed the search warrant for the illegal weapons. McVeigh stated, "I think if the sheriff had served the warrant, it would all have been okay."[4] Many people other than McVeigh noted that prior to the raid and siege, Koresh had left the compound on a frequent basis and could have been arrested then. According to McVeigh, ATF and FBI agents were inept government employees who were incapable of planning and carrying out a military exercise. And in McVeigh's opinion, being an employee for the federal government "was the unpardonable sin."[5]

McVeigh went on to explain to Rauch why he felt the federal government wanted and needed to confiscate people's weapons:

> The government is afraid of the guns people have because they have to have control of the people at all times. Once you take away the guns, you can do anything to the people. You give them an inch and they take a mile. I believe we are slowly turning into a socialist government. The government is continually growing bigger and more powerful, and the people need to prepare to defend themselves against government control.[6]

The federal government had no right to use its military weapons—such as Bradley fighting vehicles—and soldiers against its own people, he told her. McVeigh warned that the standoff in Waco was just the beginning of the government's intrusion into people's lives.

Spreading the Gospel

After a few days in Waco, McVeigh left to tell others about his experiences. He went to a gun show in Pennsylvania and then drove to Michigan to see his old army friend Terry Nichols. With the end of the siege nowhere in sight, the two made plans to drive down to Waco together to demonstrate their solidarity with the Branch Davidians. But the FBI put an end to their plans on April 19, 1993, before the two men even left on their road trip.

During the early morning hours of April 19, the FBI tried to force the Davidians to surrender by using tanks to shoot canisters of tear gas into the compound's buildings and, according to government agents, to knock holes in the walls and doors "from which the Davidians could leave the compound."[7] Then, at about noon, three fires broke out simultaneously in the compound; both the FBI and the Branch Davidians denied setting the fires. Arson experts believe the fires were deliberately set by the Davidians, although some witnesses claim they saw the tanks' gun barrels shooting flames at the buildings. The entire compound became engulfed in flames and burned to the ground. Gunshots could be heard from inside the burning structure.

McVeigh and Nichols watched the end of the siege on television in Michigan. According to Richard A. Serrano, author of *One of Ours: Timothy McVeigh and the Oklahoma City Bombing*, the two men who were watching the events unfold believed they were witnessing

> an image of warfare by the federal government against its own citizens: poison gas that was highly flammable; immobilizing tactics that locked the Branch Davidians inside the complex; heavy weaponry that broke the Davidians' perimeter and smashed their wall of resistance. . . . The government of the United States was killing its people; the slaughter had begun.[8]

McVeigh became obsessed about the events at Waco and read everything he could find on the subject. He was especially angry over the deaths of twenty-five children who had remained inside the compound. He was infuriated over the overly enthusiastic actions of the ATF and FBI agents and the cover-up that followed as the government tried to play down its role in the deaths during the raid and siege. He believed the government had trampled on the rights of American citizens with no apologies and was getting away with

it. He was determined that the deaths of the Branch Davidians and their children by the ATF would be avenged.

A Shared Frustration

From Michigan, McVeigh drove west to visit his other army
friend, Michael Fortier, who lived in Kingman, Arizona. He
discovered that they still shared the same concerns that the
federal government was trying to limit individual freedoms,
especially the right to bear arms. They agreed that the government had murdered the people inside the Mount Carmel
complex. Others also agreed with them. When the surviving
Branch Davidians were tried for the murders of the four ATF
agents, they were found not guilty. Sarah Bain, the jury's
forewoman, told an on-line periodical after the trial, "The
Federal Government was absolutely out of control. . . . The
wrong people were on trial. . . . It should have been the ones
that planned the raid and orchestrated it."[9]

During the next few months, McVeigh spent a lot of time
in Arizona with Fortier where he worked as a security guard
and at gun shows sold weapons, ammunition, flares and
flare guns, bumper stickers, and ATF baseball caps with bullet holes in them. Then, in the fall of 1993, McVeigh went
back to Michigan to visit Nichols, who was living on his
brother's farm. McVeigh was invited to live in the farm-
house, and he helped the Nichols brothers with the chores
around the farm in exchange for room and board. When they
were not working, the men passed the time by making
homemade bombs. They put household chemicals in plastic
soda bottles and experimented with different ways to make
them blow up.

McVeigh and the Nichols brothers shared many of the
same political beliefs, and so they began attending meetings
of the Michigan Militia, one of many extremist groups that
vow to defend themselves against government intrusion.
Terry Nichols and McVeigh tried to interest the militia
members in revolting against and eliminating the federal
government as well as police officers, judges, and lawyers.
The militia members thought such talk was a little too rad-

ical, however; most members joined the militia to defend themselves against threats to their way of life, not to strike first against a presumed enemy. Norm Olson, a Baptist minister, gun dealer, and cofounder of the Michigan Militia, kicked the men out of several meetings because of their antigovernment talk. "These people were told to leave because of that type of talk of destruction and harm and terrorism,"[10] Olson said. Terry Nichols and McVeigh then tried to start their own militia group, called the Patriots, with cells containing just two or three members. Evan McKenzie, a professor of political science at the University of Illinois at Chicago, explains why militia and terrorist groups prefer such small cells: "When you put together a cell of two or three people, you can keep activities to yourself and there's less of a chance that you'll be infiltrated. And nobody really knows you're out there because you're less formal and not letting people know what you're doing."[11]

The Planning Begins

McVeigh spent much of the spring and summer of 1994 in Arizona. He worked at a True Value Hardware store with Fortier but still made the rounds of the gun-show circuit. McVeigh lived briefly with Fortier and was the best man at Fortier's wedding in Las Vegas in July. By this time, McVeigh was seriously thinking of initiating an offensive attack against the government. McVeigh told Fortier that he and Terry Nichols "had decided to take some sort of positive offensive action"[12] against the government and wanted to know if Fortier was interested in joining them. Fortier was curious and wanted to know more about McVeigh's plans. McVeigh then told Fortier that the first attack would be a bombing of a government building, much like what was described in *The Turner Diaries.* Using soup cans, he illustrated for Fortier how a truck could be made into a bomb using fifty-five-gallon drums filled with explosives. At this, Michael Fortier asked McVeigh about the people who would be killed from the explosion. McVeigh responded, "Think about the people as if they were storm troopers in *Star Wars.*

They may be individually innocent, but they are guilty because they work for the Evil Empire."[13] Fortier later informed investigators that he told McVeigh that he "would never do anything like that unless there was . . . a [United Nations] tank in his front yard"[14] attacking his home and family.

During the fall of 1994 McVeigh made frequent trips between Arizona and Kansas, where Nichols had moved in order to be closer to his twelve-year-old son, Josh (from a previous marriage), who lived in Las Vegas. During those trips, McVeigh and Nichols bought tons of ammonium nitrate fertilizer. McVeigh also found someone at a racetrack who agreed to sell him nitromethane—a highly volatile liquid rocket fuel that, when mixed with the ammonium nitrate, makes an effective bomb. McVeigh and Nichols stored the bomb ingredients in rented storage lockers in Arizona and Kansas.

Around this time, a gun dealer named Roger Moore was robbed at his ranch in Arkansas by a man—believed to be Nichols—who wore a ski mask, wig, and panty hose over his face. McVeigh was well acquainted with Moore and his inventory; he had helped Moore out at gun shows and even worked for him on his ranch. Stolen in the robbery were gold and silver bars, precious stones, and between eighty to ninety handguns, rifles, shotguns, and ammunition valued at about sixty thousand dollars. McVeigh later called Fortier and told him he could make ten thousand dollars if he sold some guns for him at a gun show. Fortier jumped at the chance, as he earned only two hundred dollars a week at his job at the hardware store. To get the guns, however, Fortier would have to accompany McVeigh to Kansas, where the guns were hidden.

During the drive from Arizona to Kansas, McVeigh pointed out to Fortier a yellow Ryder truck and told him that he planned to use a similar truck for his proposed bomb. On the second day of their journey, McVeigh pulled into downtown Oklahoma City and showed Fortier the Alfred P. Murrah Federal Building and told him it was the building he planned to destroy. McVeigh mistakenly believed that the ATF agents who raided the Mount Carmel compound in Waco were based in Oklahoma City. Fortier told McVeigh his plan to bomb the building was "stupid." There were better ways for McVeigh to demonstrate his anger at the government, he said. He told McVeigh, "Stand on street corners and tell people about it. In the next ten years you'd be much more effective than doing something like this."[15] McVeigh answered that he had already tried that method—selling bumper stickers and passing out pamphlets in Waco, for example, had accomplished nothing.

Meanwhile, Nichols was in the Philippines with his second wife visiting her family. Before he had left, he had given his former wife, Lana Padilla, a package and told her to open it only if he had not returned within sixty days. Padilla believed the package contained a suicide note, and so the next day she opened it. Inside were nearly a dozen strange keys; a letter to Jennifer McVeigh, Timothy McVeigh's sister; a letter to McVeigh; and two lists of things that Padilla was to take care of immediately. In one of the notes to Padilla, Nichols wrote that he had hidden something behind one of her kitchen drawers, which was to be split between his son, Josh, and his second wife and their daughter. He also mentioned that the contents of a storage unit were for Josh. In the letter to McVeigh, Nichols wrote, "You're on your own now. Go for it!"[16] The package hidden behind Padilla's kitchen drawer contained twenty thousand dollars, all in twenty- and hundred-dollar bills. Padilla was shocked; she thought Nichols was poor. In the storage unit, Padilla found survival gear, gold coins, gold and silver bars, and stones that appeared to be jade, along with a ski mask, wig, and panty hose. When Nichols returned from his trip to the Philippines in January, Padilla immediately confronted him about the package, the hidden money, and the contents of the storage unit. He refused to make any explanations to her, and she did not press him any further. However, she demanded some of the money for Josh, and they eventually agreed she could keep three thousand dollars.

April 1995

When McVeigh first began planning his attack against the government, he deliberately chose April 19 as the day of the bombing. It was not only the two-year anniversary of the fire at Waco that killed approximately eighty Branch Davidians, but it was also Patriots Day, the day in 1775 when American Minutemen first fired on British troops in Lexington, Massachusetts, to begin the American Revolution. By the time April 1995 arrived, nearly everything was in place for the attack. The fertilizer, fuel, and detonation cord had been purchased; the blasting caps had been stolen from a military depot by McVeigh and Nichols; and the target had been chosen.

However, McVeigh was having problems with Nichols, who started having second thoughts about participating in the bombing. Marife Nichols, Terry's second wife, was upset about the amount of time that her husband was spending with McVeigh instead of with her and their daughter. With the possibility of Nichols dropping out of the plan, McVeigh turned to Fortier. McVeigh told Fortier, "I have been telling you most everything that's going on because I expected you to be there if I needed you."[17] But Fortier refused to become further involved. Michael Fortier and his wife, Lori, saw McVeigh a few times in April 1995, but Fortier continued to turn down McVeigh's requests for help in the bombing. Neither Lori nor Fortier ever notified any law enforcement authorities to warn them what their friend intended to do; they claimed later that they did not believe McVeigh would go through with the bombing if they did not help him. McVeigh was finally able to convince Nichols to continue with the plan; he told Nichols that he was too involved with the plan to back out at the last minute.

McVeigh Arrives in Junction City, Kansas

On April 14 McVeigh's 1983 Pontiac station wagon blew a head gasket just as he was pulling into Junction City, Kansas, after making the final trip from Kingman, Arizona. At a service station in town, McVeigh bought a 1977 Mercury Marquis for $250 plus the title of the Pontiac. After completing the transaction, McVeigh used a pay phone to call Elliott's Body Shop in Junction City, which also rented Ryder trucks. McVeigh, using the name Robert Kling, told the owner that he needed a truck to haul five thousand pounds to Omaha, Nebraska (about the same distance from Junction City as Oklahoma City). He reserved a truck and said he would be back the next day to complete the paperwork. Then, McVeigh took his battered Mercury and drove to the Dreamland Motel. McVeigh registered and paid for four nights under his own name, but he listed his address as the Nichols farm in Michigan.

The next day McVeigh went to the body shop, where he finalized the paperwork for the Ryder truck. He gave the clerk a false ID showing his name as Robert Kling and paid for the rental in full. McVeigh stressed that he needed the truck by 4 P.M. on Monday, April 17, and the clerk assured him it would be ready. That evening, a man called the Hunan Palace restaurant and placed a take-out order under the name of Robert Kling, to be delivered to room twenty-five at the Dreamland Motel. When the food had not been delivered an hour later, Kling called back. The manager apologized and said it would be there shortly. When the delivery man arrived, he gave the food to a man standing outside room twenty-five at the motel. He later told authorities that the man was tall with long blond hair that reached his shoulders. The description did not match McVeigh since he had maintained his military haircut even after he left the army four years earlier.

Easter Sunday

On Easter Sunday, April 16, a couple staying at the Dreamland Motel noticed McVeigh's Mercury Marquis parked in the motel parking lot. They saw it had Arizona license plates on it, and they could not believe the junker car had successfully made the trip from Arizona to Kansas. The motel manager and her son were certain that they saw McVeigh with a Ryder truck at the motel that day, which is hard to explain since McVeigh did not pick up the truck he rented under the name Kling until Monday. Eric McGowan, the manager's son, told authorities later that he had asked McVeigh to move the truck as it was blocking the entrance of a longtime motel resident. McGowan also noticed that once he saw the Ryder truck, he did not see the Mercury car any more. A woman who visited her son at the Dreamland Motel on Easter Sunday said she also saw the Ryder truck at the motel that day, as she could not see her son's car because the truck blocked her view.

During the afternoon, the phone rang while the Nichols family was eating Easter dinner. When Terry Nichols answered, McVeigh began screaming at him so loudly that Marife Nichols and Josh Nichols (who was visiting his father over the Easter school break) could hear McVeigh's voice through the phone. McVeigh was angry because Nichols had not kept a meeting with him. Nichols was supposed to follow McVeigh to Oklahoma City, where McVeigh would drop off his getaway car and then Nichols would drive him back to Junction City. McVeigh threatened Nichols and his family and told Nichols that if he did not cooperate, he would call the authorities with an anonymous tip about some of Nichols's activities. Nichols finally agreed to meet McVeigh in Oklahoma City, and now he needed an excuse to leave his family on Easter Sunday. He told them that McVeigh's car had broken down and he needed to go to Omaha to pick him up and bring him to Kansas, along with a television set that McVeigh was giving the Nichols family. Josh wanted to accompany his father on the trip; after all, his father would be gone about twelve hours, and Josh was scheduled to return to Las Vegas the next evening. But Nichols told his son that his truck would be too crowded with the three of them and the television set.

Nichols, driving his pickup truck, followed McVeigh, who was driving his 1977 Mercury, to Oklahoma City. McVeigh parked the car in an out-of-the-way spot a few blocks away from the Murrah building. He took the license plates off the car and put a sign in the car's windshield asking police not to tow the car; the owner would return soon with a new battery and cable. Then he got in Nichols's truck with the television, and Nichols drove him back to the Dreamland Motel in Junction City, Kansas. When Nichols finally returned home that evening, he found his son was waiting up for him, even though it was nearly 2 A.M.

The Final Preparation

On Monday afternoon McVeigh called a cab that drove him to a McDonald's near Elliott's Body Shop. The chain restaurant's security camera caught McVeigh on the videotape. From there, McVeigh walked the mile or so to the truck rental agency. However, some believe he may have gotten a ride to the body shop. Although it was raining, the employees at Elliott's Body Shop thought that McVeigh's clothes were dry when he entered the shop. In addition, two employees noticed that a second man had entered the shop with McVeigh. The second man was described as having a square jaw, a tattoo on his upper arm, and wearing khaki pants and a blue-and-white baseball cap. The other man did not speak while he was there. When McVeigh left with his rental truck, the time-date stamp on his receipt was 4:19 P.M.

The next morning McVeigh left the Dreamland Motel with the Ryder truck and drove to a storage unit where he and Nichols had stored the ammonium nitrate and nitromethane. Nichols was not there, so McVeigh started loading the fertilizer into the rental truck. When almost all the fertilizer had been loaded, Nichols finally arrived and helped McVeigh load the barrels of racing fuel. From the storage unit, the men drove to a nearby state park, where they mixed the volatile ingredients together in fifty-five-gallon drums. The barrels were placed in the shape of a T inside the truck—not the best configuration for the bomb—but McVeigh did not want the truck to list to one side and possibly draw unwelcome attention to it. After the men finished mixing the bomb ingredients, McVeigh wiped fingerprints off the truck, washed in the park's lake, and changed into a new set of clothes. He put his old clothes into a bag that he planned to dump later. Then he and Nichols left—Nichols for his home in Kansas; McVeigh, toward Oklahoma. McVeigh spent his last night as a free man sleeping in the truck cab in a small motel parking lot along the Oklahoma-Kansas border.

The Fateful Day

On the morning of April 19, McVeigh pulled out of the parking lot at about 7 A.M. and finished his drive south to Oklahoma City. He had originally planned on leaving later, but decided it was too risky to linger in the motel parking lot, where a nosy police officer might stop to see what he was doing. He had also considered blowing up the truck in the wee hours of the morning when only security guards and cleaning people would be in the building, but he decided against it because he wanted a lot of dead bodies for his protest against the government.

The Murrah building was perfect for his plans; it housed several federal agencies he despised: the Bureau of Alcohol, Tobacco, and Firearms, which he felt was responsible for the disasters in Ruby Ridge and Waco; the Drug Enforcement Agency; the Secret Service; and the U.S. Marshals. Although he harbored no particular animosity for the other federal agencies in the building—Social Security Administration, Department of Housing and Urban Development, the Department of Agriculture, the Federal Highway Administration, and the Armed Forces Recruiting Office, among others—they were a part of the government he hated and were therefore legitimate targets. These workers were necessary for the government to function, and therefore their deaths were acceptable.

Shortly before 9 A.M. McVeigh exited the highway and entered downtown Oklahoma City. When he was a few blocks away from the federal building, he used a cigarette lighter to light a five-minute fuse to the bomb. At a traffic light one block away from his target, he lit the second fuse—this one a two-minute fuse. The wait for the traffic light to turn green for him seemed to be the longest thirty seconds of his life, he said later. But the light turned green and he slowly proceeded to the small parking area on the north side of the building. He pulled in and parked the truck right below the day-care center that was on the building's second floor. He calmly got out of the truck, quickly walked away, and did not look back. He was about 150 yards from the building, and thinking that there had been a malfunction in either the making of the bomb or the fuse, when he heard—and felt—the explosion. He saw buildings sway from side to side, and glass from windows tinkled as it landed on the sidewalks and streets below. McVeigh arrived at his car, but when he turned the key in the ignition, it would not start. He tried again and again and again before the engine finally cranked over and he could leave the scene of destruction.

The Suspects Are Arrested

It did not take the FBI long to have a suspect in the bombing. The same day that it discovered that its prime suspect was already in custody in a county jail, its number-two suspect, Terry Nichols, turned himself in to police in Herington, Kansas. He had heard his and his brother's names mentioned on the radio as possible suspects in the Oklahoma City bombing. In talking to the police, Nichols denied any knowledge of or involvement in the bombing, but he admitted that McVeigh had told him that "something big" was going to happen soon. He refused to explain to police what he meant in his letter to McVeigh (that his ex-wife had opened) when he told McVeigh to "Go for it!" A search of Nichols's home found ammonium nitrate, a receipt for the purchase that had both McVeigh's and Nichols's fingerprints on it, guns and ammunition stolen from gun dealer Roger Moore, and a crumpled-up, hand-drawn map of Oklahoma City that showed the locations of the Murrah building and where McVeigh kept his getaway car. Although police officials eventually came to believe Nichols's claim that he was not in Oklahoma City on the day of the bombing, their evidence showed that he was aware of the plan to bomb the building.

A tip from Josh Nichols, Nichols's son, led the FBI to Michael and Lori Fortier in Arizona. In exchange for testifying against McVeigh and Nichols, the government would not charge the Fortiers in the bombing. However, Fortier had to agree to plead guilty on four other felony charges: conspiracy to transport stolen weapons, transporting stolen weapons, making false statements to the FBI, and misprision of a felony (failure to warn authorities about a crime that is about to be committed). He was sentenced to twelve years in prison. Lori Fortier received immunity from prosecution in exchange for her testimony.

The Trials

The federal government claimed jurisdiction to try McVeigh first before the state. He was charged with eleven felony counts: eight counts of murder for the deaths of the federal agents who were killed during the course of their duties, conspiracy, and two explosives charges. McVeigh's trial began in April 1997, and he was found guilty on all counts. For his crime, he was sentenced to death. His original execution date of May 16, 2001, was delayed when Attorney General John Ashcroft discovered more than three thousand pages of evidence that had not been turned over to the defense during McVeigh's trial. McVeigh waived his appeals, however, and he was executed by lethal injection at the federal prison in Terre Haute, Indiana, on June 11, 2001.

McVeigh never showed any remorse over the bombing and, in fact, referred to the children killed at the day-care center as "collateral damage."[18] His final statement was the poem "Invictus" (Latin for "Unconquered") by William Ernest Henley, which is a powerful message of McVeigh's philosophy. The poem expresses stoicism, a reliance on self, a determination to overcome all obstacles, and most importantly of all, the belief that his actions were not wrong.

Jury selection for Terry Nichols's trial began in September 1997. Nichols was charged with the same eleven counts as McVeigh, but the verdict was different. Nichols was found guilty on December 23, 1997, of conspiracy and involuntary manslaughter but was not guilty of using a weapon of mass destruction and destroying the Alfred P. Murrah Federal Building with an explosive. Because the jury deadlocked on his sentence, the federal judge sentenced Nichols to life in prison. In May 2003 a state district judge found there was enough evidence to try Nichols in Oklahoma on state charges of murder for the other 160 people who died in the explosion.

The Oklahoma City National Memorial

Almost from the first minute after the explosion, throngs of people flocked to the site of the federal building to see the destruction for themselves. They continued to come even after the building had been imploded. They left souvenirs and mementos on or near the chain-link fence that surrounded the site. Soon, survivors, family members, rescuers, civic leaders, and architects formed a task force to care for the mementos left behind and to sponsor an international design competition for the memorial. The winning memorial would honor and remember the "victims, survivors, rescuers and all who were changed forever on April 19."[19] The memorial includes elements from both before and after the bombing: a portion of the building's wall and an elm tree (now known as the Survivor's Tree) on the grounds that survived the bombing, and part of the chain-link fence that surrounded the site after the bombing where visitors left mementos for the victims. The other key components are the two Gates of Time (9:01 A.M. and 9:03 A.M.) that mark the formal entrance to the memorial; the Field of Empty Chairs that remind visitors of the 168 people who died in the blast; the Reflecting Pool; and the Rescuer's Orchard that surround the Survivor's Tree. An interactive museum, where visitors can view some of the gifts left at the site, is also part of the memorial and tells the story of the attack on the federal building. The Oklahoma City National Memorial was dedicated by President George W. Bush on February 19, 2001, just two months before the fifth anniversary of the bombing of the Murrah federal building.

Notes

1. Quoted in Lou Michel and Dan Herbeck, *American Terrorist: Timothy McVeigh and the Oklahoma City Bombing.* New York: Regan, 2001, p. 251.

2. Quoted in Michel and Herbeck, *American Terrorist*, p. 75.

3. Quoted in Richard A. Serrano, *One of Ours: Timothy McVeigh and the Oklahoma City Bombing.* New York: W.W. Norton, 1998, p. 70.

4. Quoted in Serrano, *One of Ours*, p. 70.

5. Serrano, *One of Ours*, p. 70.

6. Quoted in Michel and Herbeck, *American Terrorist*, p. 120.

7. Richard Scruggs et al., "Report to the Deputy Attorney General on the Events at Waco, Texas, February 28 to April 19, 1993." Washington, DC: U.S. Department of Justice, October 8, 1993. www.usdoj.gov/05publications/waco/wacotwelve.html.

8. Serrano, *One of Ours*, pp. 75–76.

9. Quoted in David Hoffman, *The Oklahoma City Bombing and the Politics of Terror.* Venice, CA: Feral House, 1998, p. 245.

10. Quoted in Brandon M. Stickney, *All-American Monster: The Unauthorized Biography of Timothy McVeigh.* Amherst, NY: Prometheus, 1996, p. 159.

11. Quoted in Bryan Robinson, "No Militia Patsy," ABCNews.com, June 12, 2001. http://more.abcnews.go.com/sections/us/dailynews/mcveigh_martyr.html.

12. Michael Fortier, testimony, *USA v. Timothy McVeigh*, May 12, 1997. http://more.abcnews.go.com/sections/us/oklahoma/am_transcripts0512.html.

13. Quoted in Michel and Herbeck, *American Terrorist*, p. 166.

14. Fortier, testimony, *USA v. Timothy McVeigh*, May 12, 1997.

15. Quoted in Serrano, *One of Ours*, p. 91.

16. Quoted in Lana Padilla and Ron Delpit, *By Blood Betrayed: My Life with Terry Nichols and Timothy McVeigh.* New York: HarperPaperbacks, 1995, p. 10.

17. Quoted in Michel and Herbeck, *American Terrorist*, p. 201.

18. Quoted in Michel and Herbeck, *American Terrorist*, p. 234.

19. Oklahoma City National Memorial Trust, "About the Symbolic Memorial," 2002. www.oklahomacitynationalmemorial.org/symbolic/index.html.

Chapter 1

The Victims and Their Families

Chapter Preface

S hortly before 9 A.M. on a beautiful Wednesday morning, a Ryder truck pulled in front of the Alfred P. Murrah Federal Building in downtown Oklahoma City. Most people paid little or no attention to the truck. Daina Bradley noticed the truck as she looked out the window of the Social Security office on the first floor. Bradley was visiting the office with her two children, three-year-old Peachlyn Bradley and four-month-old Gabreon Bruce; her mother, Cheryl Hammons; and her sister. Bradley thought the truck was an unusual sight since moving trucks were not permitted downtown. She stepped back from the window to tell her mother and sister about the truck. The next thing she remembered was a sense of electricity running through her body, a flash of light, and then falling and being buried by rubble. Her mother and two children were killed; her sister was severely burned by the blast. Bradley was trapped in the rubble and freed only when a surgeon amputated her leg.

Bradley's family members were three of the 168 people killed in the explosion, but her children were not the only children killed in the bombing. A day-care center was located on the second floor of the building. Of the twenty-one children who had been in the day-care center that morning, fifteen were killed in the blast. Four other children—including Peachlyn and Gabreon—who were visiting the building that morning with their parents or grandparents were also killed.

Hundreds of people who were in the building—workers, visitors, and delivery people—survived. Some escaped with minor injuries, but others, like Bradley, suffered more serious and lasting injuries. The last survivor rescued from the building was fifteen-year-old Brandi Ligons, who had been visiting the Social Security office. A rottweiler rescue dog found the teen trapped in rubble at about 7 P.M. that night—about ten hours after the bomb exploded. It took seven rescuers three hours to free her. Although rescuers kept up hope for a miracle to find more survivors, none was found during the next sixteen days, and the search was finally called off.

Trapped in the Rubble

Priscilla Salyers

Priscilla Salyers worked for the U.S. Customs Service on the fifth floor of the Alfred P. Murrah Federal Building. She was talking with a coworker when the bomb exploded outside the building. The explosion caused her floor to collapse and she fell four stories.

In the following essay, Salyers explains how she was confused by the explosion; at first she thought she was having a heart attack and was embarrassed that her coworker was seeing her in such a state. When she tried to move, however, she discovered that she was buried in concrete rubble. Salyers kept wondering why her coworkers did not come to rescue her. She describes the tremendous relief she felt when rescuers finally found her and the panic that set in when they had to leave her due to a second bomb threat. When she was eventually freed from the rubble, Salyers was amazed to see the sky where the building's roof should have been. She believes the only reason she survived and her coworkers did not was because of the grace of God.

Paul, one of my very best friends, walked up to my desk and said something. I asked him to repeat it just as the phone rang. Still looking at him, I reached for the phone with my left hand, but before I could get the receiver to my ear I was rocked by a tremendous boom. For an instant we locked eyes, then I felt as if I were having a seizure. Paul's blue eyes were the last thing I saw.

Jim Ross and Paul Myers, *We Will Never Forget: Eyewitness Accounts of the Bombing of the Oklahoma City Federal Building*. Austin, TX: Eakin Press, 1996. Copyright © 1996 by Jim Ross and Paul Myers. All rights reserved. Reproduced by permission.

Confusion

An incredible force pushed me forward and all I could see were white flashing sparkles. Loud wind rushed past my ears. I couldn't understand what was happening, and felt embarrassed, wondering what Paul must be thinking. I thought I might be having a heart attack, but there was no pain, then suddenly there was a strong jolt and I thought I'd hit my head on my desk. Everything got real quiet.

I tried to sit up but I couldn't move. I told myself to just be still for a few minutes. I wondered where Paul had gone. I expected he would be trying to help me sit up by now. I tried again, then realized there was something holding me down. I was on my stomach, with my face twisted to the right. My head was wedged tight and I had no luck moving my legs or my right arm. My left arm was free, so I reached up to find my computer. No luck. What I felt was something huge on my head and back. I thought my desk and credenza had fallen on me. I visualized Claude, whose desk is near mine, coming to help Paul get me out. The eerie silence was so loud. What was happening?

I tried to scream, only to discover I could barely breathe. The reality that I was trapped rushed home and I became extremely frightened. I started praying for survival and the will to keep calm. Earthquake victims came to mind. What had I read about them? Some survived days within air pockets, didn't they? With my left hand I began pulling rocks out from under my neck to create more breathing space. Drawing air was difficult. There was so much dust. The piece of gum in my mouth was full of dirt. I tried to spit it out, but my head was wedged so tightly I couldn't. It occurred to me that if I had suffered head injuries and my head began to swell, it would be over. I heard a voice. It was a voice of panic. "This is the child care center. We have a lot of children in here!"

Praying for Calmness

Someone answered the voice. "We're trying to get you out." This only confused me more. The day care center was on the second floor. I was in my office on the fifth floor. I thought maybe the voices were coming through the vent. At least people were there. They would find me. But where were Paul and Claude? I managed to scream for help, but with no response. I felt it would be better to save my energy and focus on staying calm until help arrived. Each time I felt myself

---

April 19, 1995, 9:02 A.M.

The blast from the bomb in front of the Alfred P. Murrah building on April 19, 1995, was felt all over Oklahoma City. People in buildings near the federal building thought the explosion occurred in their own building. Some thought it was an explosion in the natural gas pipelines; others farther away thought it was a sonic boom or earthquake or even freak lightning on a clear day. What it was, however, was a bomb made by combining ammonium nitrate (fertilizer) and fuel oil.

E xperts would later determine that the first wave of super hot gas moved at 7,000 miles an hour—fast enough that someone ten feet away would have been hit with a force equal to thirty-seven tons. In about half a second, the gas dissipated, only to be replaced by an equally violent vacuum. The resulting pressure wave moved outward, lifting the building up and causing beams, floor slabs, and connections to weaken or collapse. When the pressure wave passed, gravity took over. Nine stories on the north side of the Alfred P. Murrah Federal Building pancaked, creating a crater some thirty feet deep. People who had begun on the ninth floor ended up at the bottom of the building. Had the force of the explosion all been directed at the ground, it would have been equivalent to a Magnitude 4 earthquake; as it was the pressure wave itself was a Magnitude 1. . . .

Within seconds after the explosion, police and fire department radio channels erupted with reports, and . . . dispatchers began fielding hundreds of calls. Eventually all firefighters—both on and off duty—were called in, a first in Oklahoma City's history.

At the site, it was still, as if the world, for a moment, had

slipping toward panic, I prayed for calmness, knowing it was my only chance. I tried very hard not to think about time. I knew that if I thought about time, it would only seem longer.

A man yelled, "There's a live one!" He sounded far away, but I felt relief just the same. In reality he was not far away.

---

simply stopped turning. And then the survivors did something that captured America's heart as much as anything that came out of this tragedy: they started running. Not away from the building, but toward it, as if each person had heard someone call their name for help.

It was about 9:07 A.M., and the sky over downtown Oklahoma City was still raining glass, the shards making a delicate tinkle as they hit the concrete. In front of the Murrah building, the rows of burning cars had begun to give off a dark, billowing smoke. And the atmosphere on the street was fast becoming one of organized chaos. Rescue and emergency workers and law enforcement officials—from the sheriff's department to the Oklahoma City police—shifted into automatic pilot. They had been trained for a major disaster, and they knew what they had to do.

In the minutes that followed, some survivors simply got up and walked down the staircase of the Murrah building; others, trapped on ledges where the floor had fallen away or buried under piles of rubble, waited for Oklahoma City firefighters to find them. On the street, a few survivors picked themselves up and limped off in a daze; others drove themselves to the nearest hospital. Many more sat on curbs, staring into space or comforting others. The seriously injured were loaded—often bleeding, broken, and with shards of glass protruding from their bodies—into the beds of pickups, cars, or ambulances and driven to nearby hospitals.

A triage and treatment area was set up nearby to handle the hundreds of injured people expected to need help after the rescue was complete. That second wave never came.

Oklahoma Today, 9:02 A.M. April 19, 1995: The Historical Record of the Oklahoma City Bombing. Special memorial issue. Oklahoma City: Oklahoma Tourism and Recreation Department, 1995.

I felt his hand take mine, which was visible from the outside, and the peace and comfort that washed over me was indescribable. I heard several other men around me. They were discussing the possibility of getting me out. Someone asked my name. I took a slow deep breath and yelled out my name. He had trouble hearing me and asked me to repeat myself. It took some effort, but I said it once again, as loud as I could. He was to my left side and I was screaming into a giant block of concrete. He asked me if I knew why I was down there, then explained that there had been an explosion in the building.

Though I could tell the men were struggling in their effort to get me out, I had little doubt they would be successful. Then the same man who had given me so much comfort told me they had to leave. I squeezed his hand tight, begging him not to leave. He said they had to go for tools. It didn't make sense. Why couldn't he stay while others got the tools? I cried out and begged him to stay. His voice cracked and he said, "I'm sorry." His hand slipped out of mine and they were gone. The silence was maddening.

Trying to Escape

It seemed like hours went by and they did not come back. I finally got angry and decided I would just get myself out of this tomb. I tightened every muscle in my body in an effort to move the mountain and free myself. It didn't work. I could feel metal bars all twisted around the area I was encased in. I tried digging the broken chunks out from under me with my free hand. In frustration, I grabbed at them and threw the pieces as hard as I could. My right arm and both legs tingled from lack of circulation. I was convinced that if I could just wiggle my toes I would be okay. I wasn't in pain exactly, but I was very uncomfortable and very hot. I attempted to slip my free arm out of my jacket, but got it caught in the sleeve, so I decided to not make bad things worse.

My mind raced. The men still had not come back. I felt a lump under my stomach and reached down there, thinking it was a rock I could pull out and throw. What I discovered was not a rock, but a woman's hand. I started to cry, praying that whoever it belonged to was not suffering. I took the hand in mine and held it for quite a while.

"Just Keep Digging!"

At some point later I heard movement. A man yelled, "There's a live one!" just like before. The man took my hand into his. He said, "Just keep on praying," then he called out to others and soon I could hear them discussing the situation and planning the best way to get me out. The man asked me my name. Once again, I took a deep breath and hollered it out. After three tries, he understood: "Priscilla." When he asked my last name I refused to answer. I was worn out. All I could think was, "Forget my name. Just keep digging!"

They weren't sure how to get me out, and the more they discussed it, the more frightened I became. They brought in some chains and the "jaws of life." From time to time I could hear someone ask the man holding my hand if I was alert. Each time I would squeeze his hand as a signal and he would pass it on. After a while another man took my hand. Eventually they were able to relieve some of the pressure on my head. It was then I heard a woman crying out for help. It was the first time I'd heard another victim near me.

They were able to free my right arm, then began working on my legs. The pain was excruciating as I was forced to scrape my legs across the jagged cement in order to free them up. Next they worked on the slab pinning my head. They explained that they would need to flip me out of there quickly as soon as they had the space. It was obvious they were concerned that any movement at all could cause dangerous shifts in the tons of concrete all around.

Blue Sky

When the moment finally came, they flipped me over onto my back. I looked straight up and could see the sky. When I turned my head to the left, the sight was horrifying. I could see the extent of destruction and dozens of rescuers climbing all over the place. I also started feeling a great deal of pain. Each breath sent sharp blades stabbing through my chest. As difficult as it was just to breathe, I couldn't help but think of my friends as I looked up and could see straight through the building. I was rushed to St. Anthony Hospital, where I was treated for broken ribs, a collapsed lung, and lacerations. Scrapes and bruises covered me from one end to the other. A friend observed that I looked as though I'd been beaten up with a baseball bat.

My family, meanwhile, had been living a nightmare, not expecting to see me alive again. My son, Jason, and friend Brenda Hatfield were already at St. Anthony, waiting for my name to show up on the list of the dead. It was 2:00 P.M. before they knew I was alive. That evening, a nurse told me a fireman had called to check on me. He was the one who had held my hand and then left for tools. Later, I learned that it was the second bomb scare that had forced the men to leave. His phone call was all it took for me to forgive, and I was thankful they had chosen not to reveal the part about the bomb, as well. A few days later I met the firemen who actually rescued me. They told me I was found about four feet below the first floor. I also met the policeman who had held my hand and told me to keep praying. He told me I had squeezed his hand *hard.* I told him, "I let that first one get away, and I wasn't about to let you go!"

Few Friends Survived

While I was trapped, I had thoughts of sharing my story with all my friends in the building. Sadly, most of my friends died, including Paul and Claude, whose bodies were found several days later. After falling four floors with tons of rubble coming down on me, there simply is no answer to my survival, except that by the grace of God, I was chosen to live.

Saving the Children

Ali Hatton

> Ali Hatton was an assistant teacher at the day-care center at
> the YMCA, which was located across the street from the
> Alfred P. Murrah Federal Building. In the following essay,
> Hatton describes how the blast damaged the day-care's build-
> ing. She recounts how she tried to protect the children in her
> care and dug out those who had been buried in rubble. Most
> of the children were injured by glass and debris, and although
> one was so bloody she was not sure he would live, all fifty-
> two children in her care survived.
>
> When Hatton went to the hospital to have her injuries
> treated, she was confronted by parents who were waiting for
> news about their children at the federal building's day-care
> center. Hatton explains how she hated to disappoint them by
> telling them she worked at the YMCA's day-care center, and
> not the center in the Murrah building.

Everything was just so ordinary, like every other Wednesday morning. The three-year-olds were getting ready to
glue cotton balls onto paper cutouts of lambs. The toddlers
had just had their diapers changed, and I was sitting on the
floor in the library, leaning against a wall reading *The
Grumpy Old Rabbit* to some two-year-olds. One kid was sitting on my lap, and a few were clustered on either side of
me. With two pages left to read, I heard the loudest noise
I've ever heard and was knocked away from the wall.

The windows burst. Everything went flying—pieces of
glass, toys. The ceiling fell in. I knew there had been an ex-

plosion. Was it just our building that blew up? I didn't know. My husband, Willie, works downtown too, and he happened to be at the courthouse, a few blocks away. My mom was working about six blocks away in the tallest building downtown. Since I didn't know if we were in a war or if the whole city had been bombed, it crossed my mind that Willie and my mom might not be okay. But I couldn't think about that. The kids came first.

I grabbed the children around me and bent over them until the ceiling stopped falling on us. When everything quit moving, I started digging up the kids who'd been partially buried by pieces of ceiling. They were either crying hysterically and bleeding or they just wore blank stares and were deadly quiet. I got them out of the building by putting them through a hole in what was left of the door.

One little boy was so cut and bloodied I wasn't sure he was going to make it. His whole body was trembling. I ran to him and picked him up. I was worried that if he fell asleep, we'd lose him, so I began to talk to him about how his parents would be there soon, and I started singing the *Barney* song to him. I handed him to a medic, who then took him to the hospital.

I ended up at the hospital too. All I had was a cut across my cheek and some glass in my back. Parents kept coming up to me because they heard I was a teacher at a day-care center—they just didn't know which one. They'd pull out a picture of their missing child, and I'd have to say, "Sorry, I'm not with the day-care center in the federal building." You could see their faces drop, every ounce of hope wiped away.

I called my mom from the hospital. She was fine. I talked to my husband. He was fine. Even though I was covered in blood from carrying out the children, I was fine too and could be released that day. The little boy I had handed over to the medic had to get a lot of stitches, but he was okay.

A Party for the Kids

Two days after the blast, the Y threw a party for the children, because the last time they had seen one another, everybody was crying and bleeding, and we didn't want that image to stay in their minds for long. At the party they got to see that everybody was okay and that life was going to go on. All 52 children had survived because my co-workers and I did everything in our power to get those kids out of that building. Everybody forgot about themselves and thought about one another; mostly, we thought about the children. Less than a week after the blast, we reopened at a new location, five miles from where the downtown Y had been. We were ready to get back to normal.

It Looked Like a War Zone

Brett Brooks

Although the Ryder truck with the bomb was parked in front of the Alfred P. Murrah building, many more buildings were damaged or destroyed by the explosion. The *Journal Record* building was a block away from the federal building, separated only by a parking lot. Working inside the *Journal Record* building was Brett Brooks, who worked for the Oklahoma Guaranteed Student Loan Program. Brooks normally took his morning break at 9 A.M. in the break room at the rear of the building, a section that was closest to the federal building. On the morning of April 19, 1995, however, a telephone call delayed his break and saved his life.

In the following essay, Brooks recounts the destruction done to the *Journal Record* building. In fact, Brooks first believed the bomb had exploded in his building. He managed to escape but severely injured his ankle in the process. Outside, he describes the scene—cars were on fire, a huge crater filled the street, and blood was everywhere. Brooks found his car and drove himself and some coworkers to the hospital where they were treated for their injuries. Brooks is permanently disabled and his life has been changed completely by the bombing.

O n April 19, 1995, I was at work. I work for the Oklahoma Guaranteed Student Loan Program, and at the time we were located in the *Journal Record* building at NW Sixth and Robinson, across from the Alfred P. Murrah Federal Building.

At 9:02 A.M. I was on the phone with a borrower, which was unusual, since normally I take my first break at 9:00, and head to the break room which is on the south side of the building.

The Blast

While I was delayed in taking my break, the blast went off. It shook the building, unlike anything I've ever experienced in my life.

The blast blew me out of my chair and I landed on both ankles under my desk. When I got up, the ceiling tiles were falling down on my head and around the office. When I realized something had exploded, the first thought that came to mind was that a lot of employees were just standing in the aisles, shocked and scared. I was screaming at them to get out of there because a bomb had hit us. In fact, I thought the bomb was actually in our building, instead of across the street in the Murrah building.

Out of about 150 people in our office, most were out the door within two minutes, with the exception of several of us who were searching for injured people. I heard screaming coming from the break room area, and when I got there, I saw that the blast had totally destroyed it.

Down in the executive office, the assistant director was walking around in a daze. His shirt was completely ripped apart. He had blood all around his neck, back, and face, as well as shrapnel and glass in his back. I helped pick glass out of his back.

The fifteen minutes I was in our building I inhaled enough smoke to cause lung damage.

The only way out of the building was the north stairwell and it was heavily damaged from rubble and glass. I slipped on the way down, either twisting or snapping an ankle bone.

The Scene of Destruction

When I went outside to see if anybody was out there, I turned around and looked at the Murrah building. What I saw was something I had never seen in a lifetime, not even on television. It was unbelievable!

The building was half destroyed. When I looked in the parking lot which separated the Murrah and *Journal Record* buildings there must have been twenty to thirty cars, and every single one was totaled and on fire.

I saw one person sitting in a car on fire. I saw a couple of body parts. What I saw was devastating. There was a huge crater in the street, like some kind of meteor had hit it. It was deep and wide. You could put two Greyhound buses in that hole.

Firemen were running up and down the street. Paramedics were everywhere. Glass was all over the streets. Just about everywhere on the sidewalks you could see blood. Lots of people were wrapped up with bandages covered with blood.

I was in a state of shock the whole time. They kept telling me that I needed to go be accounted for, because they were doing a count of every employee in the building. Then I heard a second bomb threat. All the doctors and nurses, and a wave of people were running toward us and they were telling us to get back.

I did not leave. A lot of our employees were on the ground and I stayed with them. A lot of other employees also stayed.

Finally, my ankle started swelling so that I couldn't walk anymore, so I decided to get in my car. The roof was caved in, and the sun roof had exploded. The cellular phone was dead because the phones were all jammed. I loaded some of my co-workers who had cuts and abrasions into the car and we went to St. Anthony's Hospital.

A War Zone

It looked like a war zone. There were people running everywhere with stretchers, wheelchairs, and chairs. They had every kind of employee from the flower girl, to the janitor, to security, grabbing people out of cars.

When I got to the emergency room I almost passed out from the stench of blood. It was on the walls and on the floor. People were lying down, throwing up, and passing out. I told them my left ankle was hurt and they said that only seriously injured people were going to be treated. I got back into the car and headed to my hospital.

I must have been one of the first people they treated because a lot of people were questioning me about what happened and asking if there were a lot of dead people. All I could tell them was, "Get ready, you guys are going to see more people than you've ever seen in your life."

The most vivid things that remain in my mind from the day of the bombing are my co-workers screaming for help, looking at the people in front of the Murrah building who were dead, seeing all the people in the emergency room crying and screaming, and the smell of blood. For about two days I could not get the smell of blood off me.

Still Suffering

I am currently under a doctor's care. I've lost 50 percent lung capacity. I'm on an inhaler, and I take medication for water in my lungs and antibiotics to keep from getting respiratory infections. The injury to my foot and ankle required surgery. That's a permanent injury. I was told that in five years I will require a joint for my ankle.

For the rest of 1995 I missed a lot of work. I was hospitalized in June for a lung infection and an enlarged heart, and again in July for a phlebitis infection in my ankle and knee. I usually worked one to two weeks a month in 1995. I did not return to work on a regular basis until February 1996.

I have seen as many as six specialists. I currently receive counseling. I have not slept eight hours since the day before the bombing. I currently take all kinds of sleeping medication to try and help me sleep.

My life has been completely changed by this experience—physically, emotionally, and mentally. I have not seen anything good come out of this.

I see a lot of my fellow employees still suffering. I still see people jump at the slamming of doors or the breaking of glass. People cry from time to time. The employees I work with have permanent scarring on arms, faces, and legs that has totally changed their physical appearance. One employee's spouse left because he couldn't handle emotionally what his spouse had suffered.

The son of one of my employees was killed in the day-care center. That person has left the state, coming back only to handle business, but not to visit or live again. A couple of people who were injured are still completing skin-graft surgeries and bone replacements.

My employer has done everything humanly possible to take care of me and to make the work environment comfortable. I am still on light duty. However, I can personally say for me, things will never be the same.

The media so focused on the federal employees and did not have any sympathy toward anyone else, when there were many other people severely injured as well as some who were killed outside of the Murrah building.

People Helped Any Way They Could

If I had to do it all over again, I'm pretty sure I would have done what I did. The few lives I helped save made a contribution in the world. Had I not helped, they might not have been around to see their children grow up or spend the rest of their lives with family. I know the sacrifice I made and it has taken a great toll on me. I would not wish this on my worst enemy.

Oklahomans really pulled together. A lot of people who did not even know any of the injured came to the rescue with sympathy cards, money, donated blood, and donated time.

People came downtown to help out with whatever they could do. I guess it's unfair to say it was just Oklahomans, because we got a lot of help from all over the world, but basically the people of Oklahoma came to our aid.

Nobody was selfish, nobody was thinking of themselves. A lot of people risked their lives or serious injury to go back into the building. Just watching people lining up at blood banks and the hospital, as well as sending cards and letters to people they didn't even know, really was a big emotional lift.

As for the people who did this, there could not be enough

justice in the world to make Oklahomans forget.

There's not enough money in the world to buy back the loved ones, to help you get through the stress you suffered or the injuries you have sustained. There's just not enough money in the world to buy all that back.

So I would say, try and live your life to the fullest, because tomorrow isn't guaranteed.

Chapter 2

The Rescuers

Chapter Preface

Within seconds of the explosion, people began running toward the Alfred P. Murrah Federal Building to help those injured in the blast. The emergency 911 system could hardly keep up with the calls that were coming in to report the bombing. Minutes after the blast, the first emergency personnel—firefighters, police officers, paramedics, doctors, and nurses—began showing up to help in any way they could. Using nothing but their hands, the rescuers started digging through the rubble, looking and listening for survivors, but in many cases, finding bodies instead.

Some people were trapped on the upper floors of the building, unable to get out because the stairwells were either damaged or blocked. Television stations broadcast dramatic rescues in which firefighters backed their ladder trucks up to the building and then climbed up their extended ladders to where the survivors were waiting and helped them down.

A triage area was set up to prioritize and treat the wounded. A temporary morgue was placed close by for the dead. The critically wounded were treated immediately, while those less severely injured waited. Sometimes doctors had to make the difficult decision to let victims with catastrophic injuries die, treating instead those who had a better chance of surviving.

Despite the heroic efforts by the rescuers, no survivors were found after the first day. All but two of the 168 victims were recovered by the first week of May, when the search for bodies was called off. It was simply too dangerous for workers to enter the building where the two remaining bodies were buried in rubble. Their bodies were recovered after the building was demolished a few weeks later.

A Paramedic on the Scene

Melissa Webster

In the following essay, paramedic Melissa Webster describes
her reactions when she arrived at the bombed out federal
building. She was stunned by the sheer number of injured
people she saw, most of whom could not believe what had
happened to them. Webster felt guilty when she could not
give a small injured toddler the reassurance he craved. Later
she treated a woman who was near death. Webster recounts
how, if there had been more victims needing immediate attention, the woman would have been allowed to die, but since
there were few patients at that particular moment, she was
treated and lived. Despite the horrendousness of the disaster,
Webster was glad she was there and able to help those who
needed it.

I was in our management office about six blocks away
from the federal building, and I had just sat down at my
desk when—kaboom!—some of the ceiling fell in and the
glass in the garage doors was blown out. I assumed that our
building had been hit by something and ran out the door. I
was standing outside when I noticed that smoke was coming from near the federal building. At that point the first
calls for help hadn't come in, but I knew I needed to head
toward that smoke.

My partner had an ambulance ready to go. We hopped in
and drove to a spot about a block from the federal build-

ing—there was so much debris and there were so many bleeding people standing around, we couldn't go any further. As soon as victims saw the ambulance, they started running up, asking for help. I stuffed my pockets with bandages and started setting up a treatment center.

Bloodied Victims Everywhere

I've seen worse injuries but never before in that quantity and amidst such absolute emotional turmoil. Everywhere I looked I saw people with blood all over their bodies. And it wasn't fear I saw in their faces—it was disbelief.

I wanted to check on my own kids. My daughter, Dilan, is two, and my son, Dakota, is five. I wanted to call my husband, who was working about ten miles away. But after the explosion the phones didn't work.

I was starting to treat patients when someone brought over a little boy from the Y's day-care center. My daughter had gone there until earlier this year. All I could think was that this might have been my child. The boy must have been three; it was hard to tell—he had so much blood on him from cuts on his neck and near one of his eyes. Still, he was not in critical condition, so I had to leave him and help others who were worse off. But he wouldn't let go. That's when the whole thing hit me. I teared up. I just wanted to hold the little boy and cry. I shook that off. I had to. Somebody brought over the boy's older brother, who was about four—he was already bandaged—and I sent them both in an ambulance to the hospital.

A while later a medic brought over a woman in her late 20s. She'd been rescued from a building two blocks away from the blast. When I knelt down to check on her, she wasn't even breathing. But she had a real strong pulse. Her face was cut up so badly she was almost unrecognizable. I didn't want to "call" her—pronounce her dead—especially with such a strong pulse. She would have been my first to call that day. Another medic said, "You need to treat the ones who are still breathing." But we looked around and saw that, at that moment, there weren't many patients in worse

Triage

An emergency triage center was set up at the site of the bombing to prioritize the treatment of the wounded before sending them off to the hospital. Heather Taylor, a college student studying to become an emergency medical technician, arrived at the federal building with Dr. Carl Spengler. She describes how she determined how serious the victims' injuries were.

The south side of the building was the worst. Dr. Spengler decided we needed to set up the triage (an area where victims are given priority according to their condition), since no one else was doing it. More and more people started to arrive with the equipment we needed. This was the moment when I got scared. Dr. Spengler gave me triage tags and told me to follow him around and tag the people minor, moderate, critical, or dead. You would think that you wouldn't waste your time on the dead, but tagging the dead kept people from going back to them and trying to save them.

On the curb outside the building, the wounded were lined up. If they were talking, I tagged them minor; if they were bleeding severely, I tagged them moderate; if they were unconscious, I tagged them critical; and if they were not breathing, I tagged them dead.

Clive Irving, ed., *In Their Name: Dedicated to the Brave and the Innocent, Oklahoma City, April 1995.* New York: Random House, 1995.

shape, and an ambulance happened to be near, so we put her in the ambulance. Those medics gave her oxygen and got her breathing, and she ended up spending three weeks in the hospital before she went home. She doesn't know how close she came to death. If there'd been 50 other people hurt worse than she was, somebody might have had to call her.

Then there was a second bomb scare and everybody started running away. That's when I found a friend who had a cellular phone and called my husband, Todd. I said, "Hi,

I'm okay," and the phone went dead. At least he knew I was all right. After that scare was over, I went into the federal building. I heard there were people trapped inside. Kids too. I didn't even have a hard hat on. I just went in and started digging with my hands. I must have been near where the day-care center fell through, because all I dug up was baby shoes, nap cots and those low tables kids sit at. I continued to dig when someone called me over to look at something. All I could see was a woman's leg from the knee down. There was so much debris on top of her. We dug some more. I saw an arm and a head. When she was uncovered, I could tell she was gone. That's when somebody took control and said, "Everybody out." The building was sealed off, and nobody could enter it without protective clothing and gear.

The Big One

When I went back to the office that day, I saw my kids. A friend had brought them there. I hugged and kissed them, grateful that they had escaped the suffering I'd seen. They were fine. But the full impact of the experience didn't hit me until I was home, alone, in the shower. That's when I finally broke down and cried. Even then, I wasn't sure why I was crying.

In the ambulance business, you train for the Big One. You truly hope it doesn't happen, but, by gosh, if it does, you want to be right in the middle of it, doing everything you can. I'm glad I got to be there that day to help. As bad as it was, I had to be there.

Amputation

Kevin G. Thompson and Andy Sullivan

The Ryder truck with the bomb inside exploded outside the
north side of the Alfred P. Murrah building. The force of the
blast totally destroyed the front of the building. Back in the
southeast corner of the building, a slab of concrete from an
upper floor landed flat and unbroken on two adjacent piles of
rubble, forming a small cave that was about five feet high at
the opening and extended for twenty to thirty feet. The slab
sloped downward from front to back, so at the back of the
cave rescuers were forced to crawl on their stomachs.

It was at the back of this cave that rescuers discovered a
woman named Daina who was pinned by the rubble. In the
following selection, Kevin G. Thompson, a police sergeant
with the Oklahoma City Police Department, and Andy Sullivan, an orthopedic surgeon who had been called to the scene
by another doctor, David Tuggle, describe their efforts to rescue Daina. Because of the small, confined space the rescuers
had to work in, and due to the injuries Daina had sustained, it
was determined that the only option for freeing her was to
amputate her right leg.

Sergeant [Kevin G.] Thompson: A fire captain almost up
against the north wall said he had found another victim
alive, a woman. He pointed to a large pile of concrete. I
could now hear this lady talking to us. She was very calm
and did not sound as if she was in pain. I bent down and
looked but could only see a small part of her lower back. I
looked at what was on top of her—tons and tons of concrete
covered almost all of her. I felt absolutely useless, and I

knew the fire captain felt the same. It was in his eyes and face. We had only our hands, no tools to work with, but the captain was on his radio asking for equipment. I noticed debris falling; as I looked up, I could see that about ten feet above us was a ten-by-twenty-foot slab of concrete hanging by only a couple of two-inch pieces of rebar. I knew that if it fell, we would die.

Dr. [Andy] Sullivan: Only one person at a time could be in the space. We were told that if we felt any movement at all, we were to immediately crawl out. It became obvious that the woman's right leg, trapped by concrete, was totally destroyed below the knee. If we attempted to move the materials on top of her, almost certainly further collapse would occur, crushing her to death. The only solution seemed to be to amputate. Her left leg was free, as were her left arm and upper chest. I crawled down and gained access to her by lying on top of her (later I found out that both of her lungs had been crushed and that in her right chest she had a collapsed lung with blood in the lung cavity). I cut two strands of nylon rope and gradually made a tourniquet by working both of them under her right leg, digging through rubble with my hands to gain enough room. Suddenly, the firemen yelled that we had to evacuate. . . .

Sergeant Thompson: When we were told that we could go back, I went into the pit with my flashlight. I asked the woman her name, and she said, "Daina." I tried to crawl as close to her as I could. I was about two feet away, but a huge concrete beam was between us. As I lay there, I felt water dripping on me. I looked up with my flashlight and realized that the "water" was blood dripping from a crushed body above us. It was as if the concrete were bleeding. There was all this equipment beside me—jaws-of-life, power saws— and I didn't know [how] to use it. I felt so useless. I looked back up the tunnel and saw a lone fireman and yelled up to him. He came down and said he knew how to use the equipment. As he lay there assessing the situation, blood dripped onto his yellow helmet until it became a red helmet. He backed out of the hole, saying, "It looks bad." I asked his name. He said it was Jeff. In the next two to three hours in that hole with him, I grew to respect Jeff as a true hero.

Later, when the firemen had removed enough debris for me to see Daina for the first time face-to-face, I said, "It's great to see you, Daina. Hang on. It won't be much longer."

The Only Solution

Dr. Sullivan: The time outside was probably fortuitous: It allowed us to plan. Crawling back into the space, I realized the only way we could extract the patient was by a through-the-knee amputation. We had the firemen position a harness under her chest so that once the amputation was complete, we could pull her rapidly out onto a spine board. I discussed the choice with the patient. While tearful, she understood. I was fearful she might not survive much longer. She was already hypothermic, hypotensive, and having difficulty breathing.

Sergeant Thompson: A fresh crew of firemen came down and relieved Jeff, who had been working non-stop for several hours. A doctor asked me to go outside and bring him a trauma kit. I located a kit and started back down. I was stopped by a fire captain and he told me I couldn't go back. At first, I wanted to push my way down, but I realized he was just doing his job and I was tired and ready to get out.

Dr. Sullivan: Daina agreed to the surgery. I crawled back out. Dr. Stewart had selected a dose of Versed, and Dr. Tuggle crawled in and administered the anesthetic intramuscularly. Although we had some Demerol, we were afraid that it would suppress her respiration and stop her breathing. Versed had the advantage of being hypnotic and amnesic. Lying on top of Daina, I twisted the two nylon ropes with a stick to cut off remaining circulation to the leg. Using disposable blades and eventually an amputation knife, I was gradually able to work my way through the knee. Once the ligaments, tendons, and muscles had been cut, I cut through the remaining arteries, veins, and nerves at the back of the knee. The tourniquets worked so that she was not at risk of bleeding to death. We were then able to crawl out. The firemen were able to get on the harness and pull her out onto the spine board.

Sergeant Thompson: I wandered around for the next thirty minutes, looking at all the destruction. Later I spotted Jeff Hail, the fireman. He looked like a proud father. He said, "She's out, we did it, we helped get Daina out and she is going to live." It was now raining hard. I don't know why, but we hugged, and I felt like Jeff was the brother I never had. In some strange way we had bonded as if we had been life-long friends.

Honoring One of Our Own

Jim Parker

Jim Parker is a deputy U.S. marshal from Salt Lake City who came to Oklahoma City to debrief and counsel his fellow marshals following the bombing. Among the missing was a U.S. marshal, identified only as Kathy. Eight days after the blast, rescuers finally found her body. Parker described how eight members of the U.S. Marshal Service removed Kathy's body from the pit. Her body was placed on a gurney and covered with the American flag. Rescue work stopped while she was wheeled out and rescuers removed their hats and saluted as her body passed by.

Marshal Service personnel lost two family members to the bomb. A child and a wife of two of our employees died in this tragedy. It was like we had all lost two of our own family members.

I was not there when the child was located, but I was there when Kathy was finally located. On Thursday, April 27, there was news that the rescue teams might have located her. As sad as we all were, we knew it was going to help her family to find her and get her out of the building. At 4:30 P.M. I peered into the pit from up above, as a team of men and women attempted to retrieve the body of a female. We knew what Kathy was wearing on her last day at work. We also had a good description of her wedding ring and what she looked like.

Jim Ross and Paul Myers, *We Will Never Forget: Eyewitness Accounts of the Bombing of the Oklahoma City Federal Building.* Austin, TX: Eakin Press, 1996. Copyright © 1996 by Jim Ross and Paul Myers. All rights reserved. Reproduced by permission.

Soon

All we could see at first were a woman's legs and her right arm. We were in the ball game when it came to the clothes, but we could not get a look at her face nor were we able to see her left hand. We were hoping this was her, but we were not sure. The crews in the pit knew we were hoping. They would come out every so often and tell us that they were giving it their best, and that "it should be soon."

At first we were thankful that this might be coming to an end, but hour after hour we kept hearing "soon." Nevertheless, these brave men and women kept a frantic, yet controlled pace. They would dig and dig, stop and cut more metal, then dig and dig again. Never stopping, never complaining.

More hours passed. Then around 10:00 P.M. we were at last in a position to see the ring or face of the woman we prayed was our Kathy. Our supervisors, friends of Kathy's husband, gathered all marshal personnel for a briefing. We were told that if this was Kathy, we would place her body in one of those black body bags, a United States flag would be placed over her. She would then be marched out of the pit and to the makeshift medical examiner's tent by only the Marshal Service. We were all quiet during this briefing. You could feel the tension as every one of us hoped that this part of our mission was soon to be over.

The Procession

A team of eight Marshal personnel went back in for the actual extraction. I lost sight of our team as they disappeared around the corner into the pit. A short time passed and then, ever so slowly, they came back with the body of the lady we had all grown so close to. A flag was draped over her body and the gurney was wheeled to a stop.

As we lined up and started off, the rescue team that had worked so hard at uncovering her stood alongside with their masks off and their helmets over their hearts. They just stared at us. Someone stopped the procession long enough so this brave rescue team could join in to march the body out of the building and to the Medical Examiner's tent.

The underground parking garage was dark and musty, and there was dampness to it. As we exited into daylight, there stood, to our surprise, a large number of military, police, and ATF agents. They were all at attention, staring straight ahead, and saluting the flag and the lady under it. They didn't know who she was. They didn't have to. All they knew was that the body beneath that flag meant something to the United States Marshal Service. And she did.

Eight Marshal personnel entered the Medical Examiner's tent and closed the makeshift door behind them. We all then waited for the verdict. When they came out, the looks on their faces told us that we had our Kathy. No one had to say a word. We had waited over two days for this news. Though thankful, there were no celebrations, or even smiles, just a lot of tears and crying.

Chapter 3

The Aftermath

Chapter Preface

The bombing of the Alfred P. Murrah Federal Building in Oklahoma City on April 19, 1995, was, at the time, the worst act of terrorism on American soil. The explosion killed 168 people, including twenty-one children, yet the toll extended far beyond those who were killed. Hundreds of people were injured in the blast—people who were working in the building, visiting one of the many federal offices in the building, or making a routine delivery on what had been a normal day. For those who were injured, the families of the victims who were killed, their rescuers and emergency medical personnel, and for many residents of Oklahoma City, their lives would never be the same again.

Guilt was a common feeling among both those who survived the blast and those who lost a friend or family member in the explosion. Parents felt guilty for bringing their children to a day-care center, where fifteen of twenty-one children in the center died. Those who lived through the blast felt guilt for surviving when many of their coworkers did not, and they often wondered why they were given a second chance to live. In addition to the guilt and grief they felt over the loss of friends and family and the pain from their injuries, survivors also experienced post-traumatic stress, flashbacks, depression, insomnia, and anxiety, and some developed alcohol- or drug-abuse problems. Many had horrific images seared forever into their memories—seeing their coworkers or family members killed or severely injured, scenes of body parts lying amid the rubble, the temporary morgue set up near ground zero, the smells of death and destruction that lingered for weeks at the site.

Although some federal workers were able to return to work rather quickly, many others found it simply too difficult to concentrate on work. Sudden noises often frightened or unnerved them and brought back memories of that fateful day. They found themselves continually reliving their experiences after the explosion. Many could not return to work because of their injuries. For some survivors, and for friends and family of the victims, the bombing caused them to change their lives. As a way of coping with their survival, they started looking for something more meaningful to do with their lives.

Media headlines across the country were similar in their message about the bombing: "Terror in the Heartland." What many Americans found especially frightening and incomprehensible was that an American had attacked his own countrymen in a typical midwestern city—Oklahoma City—where things like terrorism simply do not happen.

Reporters Are Victims, Too

Charlotte Aiken

> Charlotte Aiken reported on the bombing for the *Daily Okla-homan* newspaper in Oklahoma City. In the following selection, Aiken discusses the effects the bombing had on the reporters who covered it—effects they felt for a year or more after the event.
>
> Despite the fact that she had been at the scene of and written about homicides and fires, Aiken was not prepared for the carnage and mutilation she saw during her first day at the bomb site. After her initial moment of shock, she got down to the business of gathering information to write her newspaper story. Aiken later discovered that her good friend's husband was killed in the explosion but she could not let herself dwell on her grief over his death. Yet the feelings of stress, anxiety, and depression that many reporters experienced had a profound effect on their lives—personal and business—and relationships with friends, family, and coworkers. Aiken writes that she discovered that life is short and that she must put her family and personal life before her work.

My friend Ted's brain ended up splattered across his desk on April 19, 1995. I stood on the sidewalk below and took notes and did my job.

I cover city hall now, but I've been both police and courthouse reporter. I read autopsies every day on those beats. I flipped through them, glanced at the grim details and tossed them aside in search of a news angle on crime and violence. That's how we survive in this business. We find it, read it and report it.

I've always reminded myself that I did not commit the murder, rape, robbery or child abuse. I simply wrote about it. I described the victim, defendant, death site, cops, judges or property owners. Sometimes I wrote about heroes. I informed the public. I moved from one grisly report to another. I kept my sanity.

Not "Just Another Story"

Ted's body was blown apart in the Murrah Building bombing. When I helped his four children write their eulogy—sitting at the table where Ted once ate—I could not forget the words in that state medical examiners report. My journalist's safety net was gone, the counselor said later.

I also try to remember that we journalists sometimes make our living off misery. But the terrorist attack on the Alfred P. Murrah Federal Building in Oklahoma City was not "just another story."

I felt guilty when I collected my paycheck that week. Ted's death and the gruesome bombing that killed 168 Americans netted me $500 in overtime pay. It also changed my outlook on life, helped end a three-year personal relationship and pushed me into therapy. I'd gladly give back the extra cash.

I have covered homicides, arson fire, police murders, gone into burning buildings with firefighters and stared down at mutilated bodies alongside detectives. None of that had prepared me for the carnage that morning at the Murrah building.

Gut-wrenching screams pierced the air. Bloodied, hysterical people poured onto the streets. Uniforms were everywhere—police, state troopers, military, ambulance crews. Firefighters in full bunker gear hung onto fully extended ladders as they coaxed the injured to safety. I will never forget the acrid smell of gunpowder. Chalk—once solid concrete wall—floated in the air. Glass shards crackled under my feet and ripped my hosiery. I could hardly breathe. People caked in blood sat on curbs clutching bandages. A deputy, cradling a child, hurried to an ambulance.

A soldier whose dress greens had been ripped from his shoulder brushed away blood pouring down his face. He tried to help a woman desperately fighting to get into the federal building. She was crying out to no one in particular and began hyperventilating. She crashed into me.

"My babies. Oh God, my babies," she cried. I put my arms around her and tried to calm her. I told her she would pass out if she didn't stop screaming and urged her to breathe slowly. The woman collapsed into my arms. The soldier and a trooper led her away.

Getting the Story

Then the news-gathering adrenaline kicked in. I grabbed people, asked questions. Kicking glass away from my pumps, I hiked my calf-length dress up to my knees and got to work. I never wore that dress again.

As the sun heated up, I stepped over broken dolls and toys scattered in the street. I knew what else had been inside—a daycare center. I scribbled notes. The debris led me to search for answers, who, what, when, where, how and above all else, why?

Many hours later our staff filed reports. Editors led them into compiled stories. No one worried about bylines, credits or beats. The pieces fell together like an interlocking puzzle.

Some time after dark my children got through the clogged telephone lines, desperate for word of their mother. This time, I did not say, "Mom's on deadline and will have to get back with you later, sweetheart."

I was plugging quotes from the screaming woman and descriptions of smashed toys into my computer when the phone rang again. It was Laurie, my best friend and Ted's wife. She wondered whether I could find out anything about her missing husband that she could share with their children. Oh my god. I had forgotten about Ted. I burst into tears. City Editor Gene Triplett walked by and asked if I was OK.

I nodded, sobbing and finished my report.

The HUD [Housing and Urban Development] office took the brunt of the blast. There was no way Ted, who worked there, could have survived. Images of him clowning on the soccer field or at school functions raced through my mind. At 6 feet 6 inches, he always looked silly ducking to get inside my house. My heart filled with dread.

For a week, until all the bodies were recovered, the medical examiner held daily briefings to release victims' names. I was sitting inside a small campus theater chatting with a Texas reporter when I heard Ted's name called. Later, I would read the autopsy report over and over. Laurie told the kids he had died quickly.

Deciding What to Report

Editors in our newsroom established a policy early on not to write gory details. We did not cover funerals. We would humanize the victims and downplay the grief. I passed on details from Ted's death to the state desk which put together the obituaries.

We struggled with the very definition of sensationalism. Was it fair to report on rescuers who may have pocketed valuables or were we harming our community image? Should we report on the woman who lost her child even though her grief led to marital problems? What was sensitive reporting and what was sensationalism?

Personal Lives Are Affected

Personal lives were at stake here—not only downtown but in our own newsroom. News people are almost as bad as the macho types some of us report on. To admit feelings of depression, fear or anxiety is to admit you can't cover the beat. We mostly keep those feelings buried deep inside ourselves.

In the past year, throughout the newsroom, personal relationships have been shaken or ended. Eating disorders and other emotional problems have developed. Use of sick time has skyrocketed. Management brought in a counselor immediately. The voluntary option was taken up by a few female reporters, but by none of the editors who experienced the same fatigue and tension reporters had.

The counselor told us that our habit of compartmentalizing stress was impractical now. Normal stress such as crime beats, deadlines or family pressures were already stored away separately in our minds. The bombing caused those compartments to overflow. The safety net was gone. It was time to deal with the pain.

Also gone was my sense of security. I resented the national media types who came into our city and made fools of themselves. I resented the federal agents who rank among the most arrogant of law enforcement types. I cried every time I saw a military humvee parked on a street corner on my beat.

I began to dread the endless bombing stories that we wrote every day for an entire year. Enough was enough. Every time I wrote something, I heard that woman screaming for her dead babies.

Ted's funeral was a news event drawing 1,200 people that I could not write about. When the eulogy was read, I knew it was among the best writing I had ever done. My writing was my gift to a friend from a skill God had given me.

I hated leaving my children each day. Although they are teen-agers, they were scared of another explosion. They know I never pass up a chance to cover the news. They know I will go wherever the story takes me. Now, they knew I could go to work and die. I hug them now more than before. For a while, I felt guiltier than I had before.

We Changed

Others were suffering, too. At City Hall, budget woes and squabbles in the administration were related to the April 1995 event. I began to question whether it was fair to report on soaring overtime at police and fire departments. These were the same cops and firefighters who had dug into that rubble until their hands bled.

I wrote my stories more cautiously. I began to bounce ideas off other reporters. When I had a question on whether or not to hammer a point about economic devastation, I'd seek advice.

But not from an editor. None of them went downtown that day. None of them saw what the mayor did on those streets during recovery efforts. None of them cried when they asked a fireman to explain why Ted's personal belongings were burnt and mangled. None of them were there when cops unashamedly cried together over a charred baby they never knew.

The staff at *The Daily Oklahoman* changed as we changed the way we did our jobs. We learned how strong our ties were to one another, but we also split into relationships according to whether we could admit our suffering or not. Those who could helped one another cope day by day.

The anniversary memorial service in April 1996 was a turning point for many of us. We had our assignments and most of us dreaded that day. More tears. More anguish. Would it never end? How much more of this stuff could we record? Reporters squabbled over who would get which credentials and who would stand where. The story developed a life of its own and it was a nightmare.

Some reporters who made it through the year didn't make it through that day. Among the most affected were a state reporter who had covered prison executions and who developed the format for the bombing obituaries, and a cop beat reporter. Another cop beat reporter cried at her terminal. Reporters and editors gathered around TV sets and hugged one another when the memorial broadcast was over. We were finally putting it to rest.

At the bombing site during the anniversary events, I watched one of our toughest photographers toss aside his cameras to step inside a perimeter to hug close friends whose daughter had died there.

Invincible

At the end of that anniversary, we compiled our reports. Like a year before, no one worried about bylines. We just did our jobs. What we turned out was one of the finest reports ever written. And we did it as a group that had been hurt together, had grown together and had healed together.

We felt invincible after that. None of us ever wants to cover another such event, but now we know we can. It's a fact. It's recorded. We still suffer from insecurities, grief and stress. But we're putting our doubts behind us and we've become stronger, better reporters because of the confidence we gained.

And I keep in mind my mortality. Like many people who lived in Oklahoma City last year, I never forget I could die tomorrow. I spend more time with my children. I put in a good, hard 10 or 12 hours each day but when I leave the newsroom now, I leave the job at work. There are other things in life even more precious than writing.

Trying to Cope

Edye Smith and Hallie Levine

What horrified much of the nation about the Oklahoma City
bombing was the knowledge that nineteen children—ranging
in age from three months to five-and-a-half years—were
killed in the blast. Edye Smith had just dropped off her two
boys, Chase, three, and Colton, two, at the day-care center on
the second floor of the Alfred P. Murrah Federal Building.
When she arrived at work, she heard a huge explosion and
raced outside to see black smoke filling the sky. She ran back
to the federal building and saw that it was almost completely
destroyed. It was then, she tells freelance writer Hallie
Levine, that she knew her two children were dead. Fifteen of
the center's twenty-one children died in the blast.

In the following essay, Smith describes how her life
changed after her sons' deaths. She and her ex-husband were
grief-stricken by their loss. They remarried and attempted un-
successfully to have another baby. Realizing that their remar-
riage was a mistake, they divorced again. Smith eventually
met and married another man and they had a baby together
in 1998. However, Smith still grieves and mourns her two
dead sons.

I was in a great mood when I dropped my two boys off at
day care on the morning of April 19, 1995. The night before, I'd taken Chase, 3, and Colton, 2, to see the house I
had bought a day earlier. As soon as we entered our new
home, they started shrieking and running through the house
like little wild animals. I remember thinking I should have
bought a bigger place, but I was just happy that I could af-

ford this one. We had been living with my mother and step-father since the previous September, having moved in three months before my divorce from Tony, my husband of five years, was final. I was so proud to be able finally to support my little family.

Both of the boys were still hyper that morning, so as soon as I got them to the day-care center at the Alfred P. Murrah Federal Building, Chase immediately ran off to play with his toy cars. I tried to kiss Colton, but he walked away. I pretended to cry, and he ran back to cover me in kisses. Chase also came back to give me a great big old hug; then on the way out, Colton ran up to me again, saying, "Kiss, kiss." It was really cute.

Awful Explosion

It was only a quick four-block walk to my job as a secretary for the Internal Revenue Service. Moments after I'd walked in, at 9:02 A.M. (I still had my tennis shoes on), all of us in the office heard a huge explosion and saw the entire sky fill with black smoke. I ran outside with my mom (she also worked in my building), and it was like entering a war zone. No cars were moving on the street and glass was falling from everywhere. I heard my mother scream, "Oh my God, the babies!" and looking up, I saw the remains of the Murrah building.

I sprinted toward the building and got there within minutes of the explosion, but a Federal agent refused to let me in. I could see rescue workers already bringing bodies out, and I started screaming for my babies. An almost supernatural feeling came over me, as if I were outside my body, watching myself plead and argue with the police. Instinctively, I knew my children were dead, and my mind went on automatic pilot. I think I was in shock. The only coherent thought I had was that I needed to get to their bodies as soon as I possibly could.

My mother heard that some of the children had been taken to Children's Hospital, so we raced there. Meanwhile, my brother Daniel, a police officer, heard about the explosion on the news and was at the Murrah building moments later, flashing his badge to get behind the barricades. He ran to the open plaza behind the bombed building and saw a row of bodies lined up on the ground. He recognized the chubby form of Colton wrapped in a blanket.

I was in the Children's Hospital chapel praying when Daniel came in to tell me. I knew right away by the tears in his eyes what he was going to say. I fell to the floor, sobbing like crazy, crying, "My baby! My baby!" Then Daniel went back to the Murrah building and saw photos of Chase's lifeless body. When he came back to tell me, I became hysterical again, but at the same time, I was relieved to know for sure that he wasn't suffering anymore. Although Chase had died instantly, I was told Colton had been alive when they brought him out of the building. His head had been crushed and there was a big hole in his stomach.

The Darkest Hours

My ex-husband, Tony, rushed to the hospital as soon as he found out, and we spent hours holding hands and crying. The next few days passed in a blur. I wept when I picked out the caskets; I should have been picking out tricycles for my boys to ride in our backyard. But nights were the worst. I'd lie awake for hours sobbing. I was also deeply upset because I'd had my tubes tied after Colton was born, and I believed I'd never be able to conceive again. I was only 23, and the thought of never holding another baby in my arms was unbearable.

My new house stood empty for two months. I couldn't bear the thought of living there alone. But I also couldn't bear staying in my mother's house, which was filled with memories of my boys. So when my younger brother, Bart, who was still in high school, offered to move into my new place with me for the summer, I accepted.

Even though my family was around, I was so lonely that I sought solace in Tony. We had initially separated—an amicable divorce—because we were polar opposites and too immature to handle our responsibilities. But Tony and I were both so depressed after the boys' deaths that we ended up getting back together. I was foolish enough to think that we could re-create the best of our old life—including our babies. A doctor in Texas had heard about my tragedy and offered to unblock my tubes for free. Tony and I both jumped at this chance to start a new family, but I should have known better. After the bombing, Tony had started going on drinking binges as a way of dealing with his grief. I foolishly thought remarrying and having more kids together would help him repair his ways and allow both of us to repair our lives. I was wrong.

We married two weeks after my successful surgery, in August 1995, just a few months after the bombing. We filed for divorce again a year later, and I haven't spoken with him since. I thank God I never conceived. It would have been a huge mistake. We were still too absorbed in our sorrow to have another child, yet we responded to our grief so differently: I wanted to make my whole house into a shrine of pictures, while Tony ripped up the boys' backyard sandbox and gave away all their toys to get rid of the constant reminders.

Mourning Becomes Perpetual

After the divorce, I thought I'd never again be able to find a man I could trust. I wanted to be alone, to nurse my loneliness and grieve for my children. Then I met Paul Stowe at the Oklahoma State Fair last September. He works as an operations engineer for Channel 5 in Oklahoma City—ironically, he'd landed his job the day of the bombing. I didn't like him at all at first: I thought he was too young (he's 23), and after my disastrous marriages to Tony, I was afraid to get involved with any guy. But Paul kept calling until I agreed to go out with him. After that first date, the two of us were inseparable. We were married this past May.

Paul is so wonderful because he embraces my past while encouraging me to look toward our future. He handles my moodiness extremely well. When I wake up in the morning crying or sob myself to sleep at night, he'll lie beside me and stroke my back. He loves it when I tell him stories about

Chase and Colton, and he sits for hours watching home videos of them. He acts like he knows them, as if they're his own children.

I visit the boys' graves once a week. Sometimes I walk around picking weeds off their tombstone; sometimes I just sit on the grass and talk to them. I like to think they know what's going on in my life. I also occasionally go down to what's left of the Murrah building. The site has an intense supernatural feeling, as if angels are all around. It's very peaceful.

We have left the boys' room at my parents' house untouched. Usually they keep the door shut, but sometimes I'll go in and look through the drawers, fingering my babies' clothes and sitting on their little beds. It's too painful for me to keep their mementos in my new house: I only keep two of their jackets in my closet. One of Colton's pockets has cookie crumbs in it, and Chase's has a little napkin smeared with cotton candy. Sometimes I go through the pockets to make sure those things are still there.

In Search of Justice

Now that the trial is over and [Timothy] McVeigh has been found guilty, I must say I feel some sense of relief. For a while, I was worried it would be a hung jury and that he would get off because it took them so long to reach a verdict. Actually, I was on a plane when the decision came in and didn't find out about it until we landed. And now that he's been convicted, people ask if I feel vindicated. The answer is no. Don't get me wrong: I have plenty of hatred for McVeigh. I've always been convinced he orchestrated the bombing and that he murdered my kids as surely as if he'd shot them on the street. The first Christmas after the explosion, I sent a card to him in jail with a picture of Chase and Colton and a note saying, "Our lives are changed now because of you." When my mother and I were in Denver for preliminary hearings, we gave him the evil eye in the courtroom for so long that he finally mouthed, "What are you looking at?" and scooted his chair away. I did get some satisfaction out of knowing that he was bothered.

Still, I no longer have the burning rage against McVeigh I once did. I view him as a crazed man indoctrinated in militia extremism. In McVeigh's mind, he's a hero: I think he's so insane, he'll never realize the enormity of what he did. I feel the same way toward Terry Nichols and anyone else involved in the bombing. But my real anger now is directed at the Federal government. I believe there is evidence that shows they knew the Murrah building was one of three possible targets to be bombed between December 1994 and April 1995. Several weeks after the bombing, my mother and I hosted a meeting for other grieving parents. During our discussion, one of the mothers mentioned seeing a bomb squad outside the building at 8:04 A.M., one hour almost to the minute before the explosion. A few of us—including myself, my mom, my stepdad, and J.D. Cash (an investigative journalist based in Oklahoma City who reported on the case)—, tracked down other witnesses who corroborated the sighting.

Real closure will not come for me until the Federal government admits to having knowledge that the bombing would take place and also apologizes to us for not alerting people to the potential danger. I'm one of 180 parties suing the Federal government now. All of us lost a loved one—a wife, a mother, a child—in the bombing. Some critics claim the lawsuit is just for money, but money's not the issue: I don't think we'll ever see a dime. What we want the Federal government to do is admit it lied.

New Beginnings

But life does go on, and now I have good news: I'm pregnant! I found out in May 1997, just a few days before my wedding. In April, Paul had accompanied me to the Pacific Fertility Medical Center in Los Angeles, where I had a cycle of free in-vitro fertilization treatments. The doctors there had contacted me when they heard about my loss and how badly I wanted to conceive again. When the nurse called to break the good news to me, I started bawling. I just couldn't believe I was actually pregnant again. Now I still can't believe God has given me another chance to have a family. I don't care if I have boys or girls or twins: I just want to be called Mommy again. [A baby boy was born in January 1998.]

Right now, I'm looking forward to spending the next few years being a full-time wife and mom. The idea of leaving my kids in a day-care center unnerves me, even though I know that's irrational. I don't have to worry, though, because I was placed on disability retirement after the bombing, so I can afford to devote all my time to my family. I'm thrilled at the prospect of watching my children develop, from their first smile to their first crawl to their first word.

Still, holding a new baby in my arms will never make up for the two boys I have lost. Sometimes, I dream I hear Chase's and Colton's voices calling me Mommy, and I can feel their little arms wrapped around my neck. When I wake up, I miss them terribly; I always will.

A jury has convicted McVeigh. But that won't bring my babies back.

A Mother's Long Goodbye

Aren Almon

One of the most riveting photographs of the Oklahoma City bombing is of firefighter Chris Fields gently cradling the body of a bloody young child. The photograph, taken by a freelance photographer, appeared on the cover of *The Economist* and *Newsweek* magazines. The child in the photo is of one-year-old Baylee Almon, who had celebrated her birthday the day before the explosion.

The following essay is written by Baylee's mother, Aren Almon, nearly two years after her daughter's death. Almon describes the anguish she has endured not only because of Baylee's death, but also because of criticism from other victims' families and survivors over the publicity of the photo. Although Almon is finally patching her life together, she still misses being Baylee's mother.

You may not realize it, but you know my daughter. She's one of the youngest victims of the Oklahoma City bombing, captured on film as an anguished firefighter held her lifeless body in his arms. That tragic image of her was transmitted around the world the day after the bloody attack. It even ended up on the cover of *Newsweek;* it was an icon of the bombing. But most people don't know how that picture has complicated my own coming to terms with the loss of my daughter, Baylee—one of 19 children who died in the Alfred P. Murrah Federal Building.

As lawyers in the Oklahoma City case select a jury, many victims' families are still wrestling with the tragedy. We are the real people who prosecutors are fighting for. Unlike some, I do not believe the conspiracy theories surrounding this case. Yes, other accomplices may be at large. But I think Tim McVeigh will be found guilty, and that he will pay with the death penalty.

That Terrible Morning

I still live with what happened that terrible morning. On April 19, 1995, I dropped Baylee off at the second-floor day-care center around 7:30 A.M. and went on to work. (I was a single mother.) When the bomb exploded at 9:02, I heard it and felt it at my desk five miles away. Then someone turned on the TV, and I recognized what was left of the Murrah building. My heart sank. I arrived at the building around 9:20. The area was already roped off, and rescuers and bleeding people were everywhere. "What about the babies in the day-care center? What about the children?" I yelled.

Soon I ran into my parents and sister. They were looking for Baylee, too. We heard that some children had been taken to St. Anthony's Hospital, where Baylee was born. Officials there sent us to Children's Hospital. Children's sent us back to St. Anthony's, where they said a baby remained unidentified. At St. Anthony's I quickly found Baylee's pediatric nurse. "Is Baylee here?" I asked. No, she said; all the surviving children had been claimed. But we heard that a baby remained unidentified? "Oh, my God," cried the nurse. "Let me get Dr. Beavers." (Up to that point I had assumed the unidentified baby was alive.) Dr. Beavers was Baylee's pediatrician. As I sat in the waiting room with my family he rounded the corner. A minister was with him. The unidentified child was Baylee, he said, and she was dead.

Anguish

We all went down to the hospital's morgue to identify her. As we approached the door I couldn't go in. Daddy went alone. I remember feeling as if the world were passing by.

The next morning I asked for the newspaper. My parents had hidden it. When I finally saw a copy, I knew why. There was the picture of the firefighter. "That's Baylee!" I said. Then the swarm started. I was afraid to step in front of my door for fear that someone would take my picture. When the doorbell rang, I froze. One reporter brought Chris Fields, the firefighter in the photo, over to meet me. I told him how glad I was that the rescuers got Baylee out so quickly, and I thanked him for holding her so gently.

Baylee was supposed to be buried on Saturday, April 22. But when Daddy went down to the medical examiner's office, they had misplaced her body. They finally found her, and Baylee was buried on Monday. I had to go out and buy her a burial outfit. That was one of the hardest things I've ever done.

Meanwhile, the photo started bothering some of the other parents who lost children. They began to criticize me in the media for getting too much attention while their children were ignored. I tried to tell them that I didn't want the publicity. But they didn't listen. When the governor suggested that a statue of Chris and Baylee be a memorial, the criticism increased. No one realized that such a memorial would have made my nightmare even worse. Criticism from other victims hurt, but commercialization of the photo was worse. Freelance photographers sold the photo rights, and the picture began showing up on T shirts, lapel pins and even telephone cards. In July of 1995 I ran across one man raffling off 18-inch statues of Chris and Baylee. "That's my daughter!" I said angrily. What was his response? He told me to buy a ticket so I could win one. The statues were the last straw. Chris and I filed suit to try to control the commercial use of the photo. A judge has ruled against us, saying I was the only person who could recognize Baylee in the picture. We have appealed.

Patching My Life Back Together

I'm patching my life together. Therapy has helped a lot. Though I have yet to return to work, I married Stan Kok, a senior airman at Tinker Air Force Base outside Oklahoma City. I really want to have more children. Before I met Stan, I asked 30 doctors about artificial insemination. They all declined—most said they didn't think I was ready. Stan and I think we're ready now. Three kids sounds about right to us. Things have slowly improved during the last two years, but I miss being a mother. I miss being Baylee's mother.

Unable to Work

Clifford R. Cagle

> Clifford R. Cagle was working at his desk at the U.S. Depart-
> ment of Housing and Urban Development when the bomb
> exploded outside the Alfred P. Murrah building. Cagle was
> severely injured by the blast but was rescued and taken to the
> hospital where he underwent surgery.
>
> In the following selection, Cagle describes the extent of his
> injuries and the surgeries he has needed. Over the next year,
> he had multiple reconstructive surgeries and still required
> more. The bombing has left psychological scars, as well.
> Cagle recounts that he is no longer able to work because of
> the stress and tension he constantly endures.

On April 19, 1995, I was working at my desk at HUD on
a solicitation that was to be mailed out the following
week. When the bomb went off, I was knocked out of my
chair by the force of the blast. Flying debris, concrete, and
glass were imbedded in my face and neck. The next thing I
knew, I was on the floor, choking on blood in my throat. I
rolled over to let it roll out of my mouth. I know I heard
people calling my name, but I couldn't answer them. I then
heard someone call my name again, and I moved my hand
so they knew I was alive. I passed out again and when I
came to, I heard another co-worker calling my name. I
moved my hand again to let them know I could hear them.
I passed out again and came to when the rescuer put me on
a stretcher. I woke up once while they were carrying me
down from the seventh floor to the ground floor, then once

again when I heard someone ask what hospital, and I told them the VA. Someone said no, so I told them Presbyterian. I realized they were taking X-rays and someone said I was all right and to relax. I didn't come to again until I was in ICU at about 9 P.M., after eight or nine hours of surgery.

My Injuries

The falling debris had crushed the left side of my skull and sliced my left eye into five pieces. My eye was hanging out of the socket by the nerve. I had lost 4.5 pints of blood by the time I reached the triage unit. While I was in the triage, the doctors and nurses thought they had lost me twice, as my heart stopped.

The nine hours of surgery were to remove glass and concrete from my face and neck. The concrete and glass had come within millimeters of my carotid artery. I also had a dime-sized hole in my skull, and the doctors thought I might have brain damage. Glass had penetrated the membrane between my skull and brain.

My wife did not know about the bombing because she was running errands. When she arrived home, she turned the television on, not paying much attention to it, until they said the Murrah Federal Building had been bombed. She called me but could not get an answer.

My daughter told my wife that they needed to go to the hospital to try and find me. My wife said, "No, I think we should stay here so someone can get in touch if they have to."

Around 11 A.M., my youngest daughter called from school in a hysterical state, so my wife went to the high school and picked her up.

My Surgeries

About noon, the hospital called my wife and told her I was in surgery and would be there for several hours and cautioned her not to hurry.

On the following Tuesday, I had another three hours of surgery to have my left eye removed and a prosthesis inserted, which was made of natural coral.

On April 25, 1995, I had another nine hours of surgery, this time to reconstruct the left side of my skull. The surgeon said my forehead was like putting a jigsaw puzzle together.

While I was in the hospital, some of the Dallas Cowboys players came to see me, including Michael Irving. I was joking around with him about being homeboys because I was from Florida also. After he left, the PR person for the hospital told me that Michael had invited me to a Cowboys game.

In May, I was fitted with a new prosthesis for my left eye. I also had to wear a mask to help reshape my eye and face. For a period of three months, and after all of my other surgeries, I had to go back every other day to have the mask reshaped.

In September, I had two more surgeries to tie the nerves back together on the left side of my face.

In December, I had eight teeth pulled to correct the jaw joint of the left side of my face because it had been damaged and the only way to correct it was to correct my overbite. So, I have to wear braces to straighten my teeth. Then my jaw will have to be broken to remove some of the jawbone.

In May 1996, I had another four hours of reconstructive surgery to fill in where the surgeons had cut some of my skull bone to use to reform my eye socket.

My eye doctor was to do some surgery on my eye also, but I believe he will do it all at once when I have my jaw surgery.

I went back to work in October 1995 and worked until November 1996. I can't stand the tension of going to work. I have a knot in my shoulder all day, my right arm is numb, and my neck is so tight it hurts. I was advised to take some leave to get away from the office. I am now applying for medical retirement because I cannot work with this much tension.

Good Can Overcome Evil

Bill Clinton

Bill Clinton was the forty-second president of the United States. He and his wife, Hillary Rodham Clinton, visited Oklahoma City shortly after the bombing to participate in a memorial service. In 1996 the Clintons returned to Oklahoma City for the one-year anniversary of the bombing. The following reading is an excerpt of his speech at that memorial service in which he consoled the victims' families and commended them for their actions which prove that good can overcome evil.

President Clinton praised them for their strength, courage, and faith and urged them to continue their efforts to rebuild. The citizens of Oklahoma, he asserted, have drawn the nation closer together and have shown that even the most tragic disasters cannot extinguish the hope and love that is within each person.

I come here today as much as anything else to thank you. On this very difficult and painful day for me, when I have lost a great and good friend and a lot of gifted employees of the Federal Government, some of them very young, and some wonderful members of our Armed Forces and some of our Nation's most able business leaders, the power of your example is very much with me, and I thank you for that.

A year ago we were here to join in mourning your loss and praying for your healing. Today I ask that we not only

Bill Clinton, remarks to the families of the victims of the 1995 bombing in Oklahoma City, April 5, 1996.

remember your loss but celebrate the rebuilding you have already done and the work you will still do.

I have relived the moments of last year many times in my mind since I was here with you. I have wondered how you were doing and prayed for your strength. I was honored to have two of your citizens at the State of the Union Address and to recognize their unique contributions to our country through their service to you.

Just a few moments ago I was honored to lay a wreath, along with the First Lady and some children who survived and their parents, and then to dedicate the child care center that will be built near the site of the bombing, thanks to the remarkable efforts of your public officials and private citizens together. You have shown how strong you are, and you have given us all an example of the power of faith and community, the power of both God's grace and human courage.

Good Can Overcome Evil

On this Good Friday, what you have done has demonstrated to a watching and often weary and cynical world that good can overcome evil, that love can outlast hate, that the light of human life can shine on through the most terrible darkness. And so I thank you for that. And I know that you could not have done it without your faith.

On this Friday I can't help noting that there is a wonderful verse in the Book of Matthew which says that a person who follows the word of God will be likened unto a wise man who built his house on a rock. And the rain descended and the floods came and the winds blew and beat upon the house, and it fell not, for it was founded upon a rock. Well your building was blown down, and many lives were shattered. But today, I saw again that the spirit of Oklahoma City fell not, for it is founded upon a rock. And I thank you for showing that to America.

From the early rescue efforts that so many engaged in to the scholarship funds for the children who lost their parents, to the current outpouring of support that will enable families to travel to Denver for the trial, to the dedication ceremony I just attended, I see over and over and over again that you have redeemed the promise of essential human nature and human possibility that we celebrate so profoundly in this season. And what I want [you] to know is that, in doing that, you have renewed the faith of America. You have drawn our national family closer together.

A year ago I was able to come here and say to you that you have lost too much, but you have not lost everything. You have not lost America. In the year since, America has stood with you and prayed with you and worked with you as you rebuild. But today, I come to you to say you have given America something precious, a greater sense of our shared humanity, our common values, our obligations to one another. You've taken some of the meanness out of our national life and put a little more love and respect into it, in ways that you probably cannot even imagine. And I thank you for that.

I will call on all Americans to express their solidarity with you when you celebrate the first anniversary of your tragedy. Earlier today I signed a proclamation calling for a moment of silence across our land on April the 19th at 9:02 A.M., Central Daylight Time, to ask the American people to gather in silent prayer and quiet reflection with their friends and neighbors, wherever they live, from Maine to Alaska, to southern California, to Florida.

In Memory of the Dead

And let me say to all of you again, we will be there with you. But because of what you have felt and what you have endured, let me ask you now if you will bow your heads in silent prayer to remember all that this year has meant to you and to pray for those who lost their loved ones on that plane in Bosnia. [An Air Force plane carrying U.S. Secretary of Commerce Ron Brown and thirty-four others crashed April 3, 1996, killing all aboard.] Only you can know how they feel.

May we pray.

[At this point, a moment of silence was observed.]

Amen.

I would like to say a special word now to some of the people who were involved here a year ago: To the Federal workers who survived the blast and are back on the job, we're glad, and we support you. To those who are not yet back on the job, we will stand with you until the day you are able to work again. To those who lost their lives in the service of their country, trying to help America get through every day in the best possible way, we thank you, your families, beyond measure.

Before Hillary and I left the White House this morning, we planted a new dogwood tree on the South Lawn to honor the memory of those who died in the crash in Bosnia. It is very near the one we planted a year ago, before we came to be with you for the first time, in honor of the loved ones that you lost. A year ago I noted that the dogwood tree embodies the lesson of the Psalms, that the life of a good person is like a tree whose leaf does not wither; that just as a tree takes a long time to grow, sometimes wounds take a long time to heal. Well, your tree has taken root on the South Lawn of the White House. In a few weeks it will flower. The healing power of our faith has also taken root and must bloom again here.

Miracles

You know, this Easter Sunday all over the world the over 1.5 billion people who are Christians will be able to bear witness to our faith that the miracles of Jesus and the miracles of the human spirit in Oklahoma City only reflect the larger miracle of human nature that there is something eternal within each of us, that we all have to die and that no bomb can blow away even from the littlest child that eternity which is within each of us.

I know a lot of you are still hurting, but I hope as Sunday comes you'll be able to find some comfort in that. Your healing has to go on. A lot of you probably still have your doubts about all of this. I'm sure there's some lingering anger and even some rage and dark and lonely nights for many of the family members. I can only say to you that the older I get the more I know that we have to try harder to make the most of each day and accept the fact that things will happen we can never understand or justify.

We flew over my home State, you know, coming here, and it made me think of the words of an old Gospel song that were actually written in Arkansas. And I thought I would leave you with these words, and our love and respect, as we move toward Easter.

The hymn goes: "Further along we'll know all about it. Further along we'll understand why. Rise up, my brothers, and walk in the sunshine. Further along we'll understand why."

God bless you, and God bless America.

Chapter 4

Understanding Timothy McVeigh

Chapter Preface

W hen Americans heard that the Alfred P. Murrah Federal Building in Oklahoma City had been bombed, many assumed the bombing was the act of Islamic terrorists. In 1993 just two years earlier, Islamic terrorists had bombed the World Trade Center in New York City, and many Americans believed the Oklahoma City bombing was another foreign attack against their country. When Timothy McVeigh was arrested for the bombing, millions of Americans were shocked that a white American male—who had proudly served in the U.S. Army—could hate his government so much that he would murder and injure hundreds of innocent men, women, and children.

Part of the motivation behind McVeigh's actions was the anger he felt toward federal law enforcement agencies. The FBI and the Bureau of Alcohol, Tobacco, and Firearms (ATF) had botched two high-profile cases in 1992 and 1993, leading to the unnecessary deaths of civilians. At Ruby Ridge, Idaho, an undercover federal agent had convinced Randy Weaver to sell him a sawed-off shotgun. When Weaver refused to become an informant against a nearby white supremacist group, the U.S. marshal arrived with an arrest warrant. When the family dog alerted Weaver to the presence of strangers, the federal agents shot and killed it. Weaver's fourteen-year-old son, Sammy, shot at the intruders, and he was shot in the back and killed as he ran toward the family cabin. A U.S. marshal, William Degan, was shot and killed by a family friend of the Weavers, Kevin Harris, who saw Sammy die in front of him. The next day Weaver's wife, Vicki, was shot and killed as she stood in the cabin's doorway holding the couple's ten-month-old daughter. For the next eleven days, four hundred law enforcement agents from the FBI, ATF, U.S. Marshals Service, National Guard, and local and state police surrounded the cabin until Weaver surrendered. He was eventually acquitted of all charges, except the original weapons charge.

The second incident was the federal siege at the compound of a religious cult in Waco, Texas. The Branch Davidians, led by David Koresh, had a stockpile of weapons, including some outlawed by the federal government. ATF agents arrived at the compound on February 28, 1993, with a search warrant for the illegal weapons. A gun battle broke out, and four federal agents and six cult members were killed. The FBI then arrived and took charge, beginning a siege that lasted fifty-one days. On April 19, 1993, the FBI sent in a tank to knock down the compound's walls. Fires broke out simultaneously around the compound. In the end, Koresh and about seventy-five to eighty of his followers were killed (accounts vary on the total number killed).

McVeigh was convinced that Ruby Ridge and Waco were not isolated incidents illustrating governmental abuse of power. In his view, they were just two in a long string of abuses. His anger over the government's cavalier and arrogant attitude toward citizens who upheld the Second Amendment's guarantee of the right to bear arms eventually led him to the belief that he had to strike back at the government.

A Person Like Anyone Else

Timothy McVeigh, interviewed by Patrick E. Cole

Timothy McVeigh was quickly identified as the main suspect in the Oklahoma City bombing. Two days after the bombing, federal authorities discovered McVeigh was already in custody in a small town about eighty miles from Oklahoma City. He had been arrested shortly after the bombing and held in jail on traffic and weapons charges. Federal agents brought McVeigh back to Oklahoma City where he was charged with the bombing of the Alfred P. Murrah building and the murder of 168 people. He was held in a federal prison in Oklahoma for the next year until he was moved to Colorado for trial because of extensive publicity in Oklahoma City.

A day before his move to Colorado, McVeigh gave an interview to Patrick E. Cole, a reporter for *Time* magazine. McVeigh maintained throughout the interview that he was innocent of the bombing. He was not the monster that some made him out to be; he liked the same things as everyone else.

TIME: You have been painted as a kid from a working-class family who somewhere along the line became disenchanted with the government and became involved in the bombing. Are you the killer people think you are?

McVeigh: If it means that I was angered at Waco and I enjoy guns as a hobby, I do go to gun shows, and I follow the beliefs of the Founding Fathers. If it means that I was involved in the bombing, then that means about a billion other Ameri-

Patrick E. Cole, "'I'm Just Like Anyone Else': An Exclusive Interview with Timothy McVeigh," *Time*, vol. 147, April 15, 1996, p. 56. Copyright © 1996 by Time, Inc. Reproduced by permission.

cans were involved as well. I don't think it is right to take someone's beliefs and convict them because of those beliefs.

TIME: What do you think about the prosecution's case against you?

McVeigh: While I can't discuss the specific evidence, people have to realize that 90% of the case that people think they have, it has all been through nonverifiable leaks. And I think you would be surprised how much those leaks are bogus. Especially through eyewitnesses.

TIME: Have you ever built a bomb?

McVeigh: I've never had my hand on one. I used to watch other people do it. I won't go into that. There were plastic soda bottles. They would put vinegar and baking soda in and screw the cap on, and it would burst.

"I'm Just Like Anyone Else"

TIME: Who is Timothy McVeigh? Who are you? What moves you?

McVeigh: I don't think there is any way to narrow my personality down and label it as one thing or another. I'm just like anyone else. Movies I enjoy, comedies, sci fi. The big misconception is that I'm a loner. Well, I believe in having my own space. But that in no way means I'm a loner. I like women, social life. I don't think there is anything wrong with that.

TIME: People believe The Turner Diaries *was an inspiration for the Oklahoma City bombing. You had this book, right?*

McVeigh: I bought the book out of the publication that advertised the book as a gun-rights book. That's why I bought it; that's why I read it. In fact, I just recently read an interview with another Army buddy who said the same thing, that Tim gave me that book and told me to ignore the parts that were too extreme.

Thoughts About the Trial

TIME: Are you satisfied with Judge Matsch based on what you've read about him?

McVeigh: And what I've seen of him. I'm impressed with the man. I like him. My view is that he is objective. He criticizes the prosecution as much as the defense. He's not pulling favorites. I even like his sense of humor.

TIME: Why do you want to take the stand at your upcoming trial?

McVeigh: So that the jurors know me and not what they've read.

TIME: What do you ask of the jury that will be selected in Denver to judge you?

McVeigh: I know it's human nature to not ignore what you've heard in the press, but I would ask them to be objective and open-minded. I have been misunderstood through labeling. Speed freak. Gun freak. Loner. My defense attorneys have said that people they have interviewed give a completely different picture of me.

In Your Defense

TIME: When people look at the Oklahoma bombing situation, most people in Oklahoma say that "based on what I've read, McVeigh had some involvement." If you could talk to the people in Oklahoma City, what would you tell them in your defense?

McVeigh: I think we know exactly what we're going to tell them, but we're going to save it for court. Judge Matsch doesn't want this tried in the press, and I agree with that. But I believe in offsetting the demonization characteristics they put out. I believe that it is an accurate response and a just response.

TIME: Can you tell us this then: If you weren't in Oklahoma City the morning of the bombing, where were you?

McVeigh: I can't tell you. We're saving that for trial.

TIME: What do you think about Janet Reno's and President Clinton's calling for the death penalty for the suspects in the bombing before the investigation had been completed?

McVeigh: I thought it was awfully hypocritical, especially because in some ways, the government was responsible for doing it. I thought she was playing both sides of the fence.

TIME: What would be your principal complaint about the FBI?

McVeigh: Their actions in Waco, Texas, were wrong. And I'm not fixated on Waco. It's a very good example of things they have done. Like leaks of false allegations. If I could meet with FBI Director Louis Freeh, I would tell him we better order out pizza because it's going to be a lengthy meeting.

TIME: We understand you've seen a psychiatrist in the past eight weeks.

McVeigh: In the last couple of weeks. The conditions were getting to me. A camera 20 hours a day on you, and then you have a guy sitting 4 or 5 ft. away from you. I'm in a 15-ft. by 15-ft. cage. You can't run. You can't do sit-ups. There is no other way to vent. I had no way of getting rid of my stress.

"Not Guilty"

TIME: Why don't you come out and maintain your innocence?

McVeigh: I have, and I've said I'm not guilty.

A Likeable Man

Theodore Kaczynski

After Timothy McVeigh was convicted of the Oklahoma City bombing, he was sent to a high-security federal prison in Florence, Colorado, to wait out his time until his execution. The "Supermax" prison was home to three other notorious prisoners: Theodore Kaczynski, also known as the Unabomber for sending bombs through the mail; Ramzi Ahmed Yousef, convicted of being the mastermind behind the World Trade Center bombing in 1993; and Luis Felipe, a leader of the extremely violent New York Latin Kings gang who continued to send orders to his gang while in prison before he was sent to the Supermax. The three men were isolated from each other and confined to their cells for twenty-three hours a day. Several months after his arrival at Supermax, McVeigh and the other three prisoners were allowed to exercise outside at the same time—although in separate cages. It was during this period that McVeigh discovered he had much in common with Kaczynski. They both had similar political views and felt disdain for federal law enforcement officials.

Kaczynski wrote a letter to the authors of a book about McVeigh in which he gave his impressions of the Oklahoma City bomber. He thought McVeigh was a very likeable person and intelligent, although he did not agree with McVeigh's protest against the U.S. government. He believed McVeigh could have registered his anger against the government in a way that did not harm innocent civilians. However, Kaczynski believed there were other incidents that were more horrifying—and that killed more innocent people—than the Oklahoma City bombing. The loss of thousands of lives was accepted, however, Kaczynski maintained, because the killers were the U.S. government and its agents.

I should begin by noting that the validity of my comments about McVeigh is limited by the fact that I didn't know him terribly well. We were often put in the outdoor rec yard together in separate wire-mesh cages, but I always spent most of the rec period running in a small oval, because of the restricted area of the cages and consequently I had only about 15 or 20 minutes of each rec period for talking with other inmates. Also, I was at first reluctant to become friendly with McVeigh because I thought (correctly) that any friendly relations between McVeigh and me would be reported to the media and I also thought (incorrectly, it seems) that such reports would lose me many supporters. But my reluctance very soon passed away: When you're confined with other people under the conditions that exist on this range of cells, you develop a sense of solidarity with them regardless of any differences or misgivings.

A Likeable Man

On a personal level I like McVeigh and I imagine that most people would like him. He was easily the most outgoing of all the inmates on our range of cells and had excellent social skills. He was considerate of others and knew how to deal with people effectively. He communicated somehow even with the inmates on the range of cells above ours, and, because he talked with more people, he always knew more about what was going on than anyone else on our range.

Another reason why he knew more about what was going on was that he was very observant. Up to a point, I can identify with this trait of McVeigh's. When you've lived in the woods for a while you get so that your senses are far more alert than those of a city person; you will hardly miss a footprint, or even a fragment of one, and the slightest sound, if it deviates from the pattern of sounds that you're expecting to hear at a given time and place, will catch your attention.

But when I was away from the woods, or even when I was in my cabin or absorbed in some task, my senses tended to turn inward, so to speak, and the observant alertness was shut off. Here at the ADX [short for Administrative Maximum, the Supermax prison where Kaczynski and McVeigh were held], my senses and my mind are turned inward most of the time, so it struck me as remarkable that even in prison McVeigh remained alert and consistently took an interest in his surroundings.

It is my impression that McVeigh is very intelligent. He thinks seriously about the problems of our society, especially as they relate to the issue of individual freedom, and to the extent that he expressed his ideas to me they seemed rational and sensible. However, he discussed these matters with me only to a limited extent and I have no way of being sure that he does not have other ideas that he did not express to me and that I would not consider rational or sensible. I know almost nothing about McVeigh's opinions concerning the U.S. government or the events at Waco and Ruby Ridge. Someone sent me a transcript of his interview with *60 Minutes*, but I haven't read it yet. Consequently, I have no way of knowing whether I would consider his opinion on these subjects to be rational or sensible.

The Far Right

McVeigh is considered to belong to the far right, and for that reason some people apparently assume that he has racist tendencies. But I saw no indication of this. On the contrary, he was on very friendly terms with the African-American inmates here and I never heard him make any remark that could have been considered even remotely racist. I do recall his mentioning that prior to the Gulf War, he and other soldiers were subjected to propaganda designed to make them hate the people they were going to fight, but when he arrived in the Persian Gulf area he discovered that the "enemies" he was supposed to kill were human beings just like himself, and he learned to respect their culture.

McVeigh told me of his idea (which I think may have significant merit) that certain rebellious elements on the American right and left respectively had more in common with one another than is commonly realized, and that the two groups ought to join forces. This led us to discuss, though only briefly, the question of what constitutes the "right." I pointed out that the word "right," in the political sense, was originally associated with authoritarianism, and I raised the question of why certain radically anti-authoritarian groups (such as the Montana Freemen) were lumped together with authoritarian factions as the "right." McVeigh explained that the American far right could be roughly divided into two branches, the fascist/racist branch, and the individualistic or freedom-loving branch which generally was not racist. He did not know why these two branches were lumped together as the "right," but he did suggest a criterion that could be used to distinguish left from right: the left (in America today) generally dislikes firearms, while the right tends to be attracted to firearms.

By this criterion McVeigh himself would have to be assigned to the right. He once asked me what kind of rifle I'd used for hunting in Montana, and I said I'd had a .22 and a .30-06. On a later occasion McVeigh mentioned that one of the advantages of a .30-06 was that one could get armor-piercing ammunition for it. I said, "So what would I need armor-piercing ammunition for?" In reply, McVeigh indicated that I might some day want to shoot at a tank. I didn't bother to argue with him, but if I'd considered it worth the trouble I could have given the obvious answer: that the chances that I would ever have occasion to shoot at a tank were very remote. I think McVeigh knew well that there was little likelihood that I would ever need to shoot at a tank—or that he would either, unless he rejoined the Army. My speculative interpretation is that McVeigh resembles many people on the right who are attracted to powerful weapons for their own sake and independently of any likelihood that they will ever have a practical use for them. Such people tend to invent excuses, often far-fetched ones, for acquiring weapons for which they have no real need.

But McVeigh did not fit the stereotype of the extreme right-wingers. I've already indicated that he spoke of respect for other people's cultures, and in doing so he sounded like a liberal. He certainly was not a mean or hostile person, and I wasn't aware of any indication that he was super patriotic. I suspect that he is an adventurer by nature, and America since the closing of the frontier has had little room for adventurers.

The Oklahoma City Bombing

McVeigh never discussed the Oklahoma City bombing with me, nor did he ever make any admissions in my hearing. I know nothing about that case except what the media have said, so I'm not going to offer any opinion about whether McVeigh did what they say he did. However, assuming that the Oklahoma City bombing was intended as a protest against the U.S. government in general and against the government's actions at Waco in particular, I will say that I think the bombing was a bad action because it was unnecessarily inhumane.

A more effective protest could have been made with far less harm to innocent people. Most of the people who died at Oklahoma City were, I imagine, lower-level government employees—office help and the like—who were not even remotely responsible for objectionable government policies or for the events at Waco. If violence were to be used to express protest, it could have been used far more humanely, and at the same time more effectively, by being directed at the relatively small number of people who were personally responsible for the policies or actions to which the protesters objected. Such protest would have attracted just as much national attention as the Oklahoma City bombing and would have involved relatively little risk to innocent people. Moreover, the protest would have earned far more sympathy than the Oklahoma City bombing did, because it is safe to assume that many anti-government people who might have accepted violence that was more limited and carefully directed were repelled by the large loss of innocent life at Oklahoma City.

Far Greater Horrors

The media teach us to be horrified at the Oklahoma City bombing, but I won't have time to be horrified at it as long as there are greater horrors in the world that make it seem insignificant by comparison. Moreover, our politicians and our military kill people in far larger numbers than was done at Oklahoma City, and they do so for motives that are far more cold blooded and calculating. On orders from the president, a general will kill some thousands of people (usually including many civilians regardless of efforts to avoid such losses) without bothering to ask himself whether the killing is justified. He has to follow orders because his only other alternative would be to resign his commission, and naturally he would rather kill a few thousand people than spoil his career. The politicians and the media justify these actions with propaganda about "defending freedom." However, even if America were a free society (which it is not), most U.S. military action during at least the last couple of decades has not been necessary for the survival of American society but has been designed to protect relatively narrow economic or political interests or to boost the president's approval rating in the public-opinion polls.

The media portray the killing at Oklahoma City as a ghastly atrocity, but I remember how they cheered the U.S. action in the Gulf War just as they might have cheered for their favorite football team. The whole thing was treated as if it were a big game. I didn't see any sob stories about the death agonies of Iraqi soldiers or about their grieving families. It's easy to see the reason for the difference: America's little wars are designed to promote the interests of "the system," but violence at home is dangerous to the system, so the system's propaganda has to teach us the correspondingly correct attitudes toward such events. Yet I am much less repelled by powerless dissidents who kill a couple hundred because they think they have no other way to effectively state their protest, than I am by politicians and generals—people in positions of great power—who kill hundreds or thousands for the sake of cold calculated political and economic advantages.

Federal Law Enforcement Officers

You asked for my thoughts on the behavior of federal law enforcement officers. My personal experience suggests that federal law enforcement officers are neither honest nor competent, and that they often disobey their own rules.

I've found by experience that any communication with journalists is risky for one in my position. I'm taking the risk in this case mainly because I think that McVeigh would want me to help you in the way that I have. As I indicated near the beginning of this letter, when you're locked up with other people you develop a sense of solidarity with them in spite of any differences.

Sincerely yours, Ted Kaczynski

An Essay on Hypocrisy

Timothy McVeigh

> Although Timothy McVeigh finally conceded after his conviction that he did indeed bomb the federal building in Oklahoma City, he continued to assert that he was unaware there was a day-care center inside the building. He angered many Americans when he referred to the children who were killed in the blast as "collateral damage," a military term that refers to innocent civilians killed by accident during wartime.
>
> Despite the deaths of nineteen children, McVeigh never veered from considering his assault against the federal building as an attack against an enemy government in which civilian deaths, while regrettable, were necessary. In an article written for *Media Bypass*, an alternative publication that supports the militia movement, McVeigh compared the bombing of the Murrah federal building to America's military policy against Iraq in the years following the Gulf War. McVeigh contends that America's policy is extremely hypocritical. American military and political leaders assert that day-care centers in Iraqi government centers are used as "shields" while day-care centers in American government buildings are there for the employees' convenience. In addition, he maintains that Americans do not protest their government's decision to kill Iraqi government workers simply because they work for the government, but this logic does not extend to American government workers who were killed in the Oklahoma City bombing. He concludes that when Americans approve of the morality of killing foreigners in wartime they have no right to object to the killing of Americans.

The [Clinton] administration has said that Iraq has no right to stockpile chemical or biological weapons ("weapons of mass destruction")—mainly because they have used them in the past.

The United States Sets the Precedent

Well, if that's the standard by which these matters are decided, then the U.S. is the nation that set the precedent. The U.S. has stockpiled these same weapons (and more) for over 40 years. The U.S. claims that this was done for deterrent purposes during the "Cold War" with the Soviet Union. Why, then is it invalid for Iraq to claim the same reason (deterrence)—with respect to Iraq's (real) war with, and the continued threat of, its neighbor Iran?

The administration claims that Iraq has used these weapons in the past. We've all seen the pictures that show a Kurdish woman and child frozen in death from the use of chemical weapons. But, have you ever seen these pictures juxtaposed next to pictures from Hiroshima or Nagasaki?

I suggest that one study the histories of World War I, World War II and other "regional conflicts" that the U.S. has been involved in to familiarize themselves with the use of "weapons of mass destruction."

Remember Dresden? How about Hanoi? Tripoli? Baghdad? What about the big ones—Hiroshima and Nagasaki? (At these two locations, the U.S. killed at least 150,000 non-combatants—mostly women and children—in the blink of an eye. Thousands more took hours, days, weeks, or months to die.)

If [Iraqi leader] Saddam [Hussein] is such a demon, and people are calling for war crimes charges and trials against him and his nation, why do we not hear the same cry for blood directed at those responsible for even greater amounts of "mass destruction"—like those responsible and involved in dropping bombs on the cities mentioned above?

The truth is, the U.S. has set the standard when it comes to the stockpiling and use of weapons of mass destruction.

Hypocrisy when it comes to death of children? In Oklahoma City, it was family convenience that explained the presence of a day-care center placed between street level and the law enforcement agencies which occupied the upper floors of the building. Yet when discussion shifts to Iraq, any day-care center in a government building instantly becomes "a shield." Think about that.

(Actually, there is a difference here. The administration has admitted to knowledge of the presence of children in or

---

The Turner Diaries

The Turner Diaries *was written in 1978 by Andrew Mac-Donald, a pseudonym of William Pierce, the former leader of a white supremacist group. The novel is the purported diary of Earl Turner, a soldier and martyr of a twentieth-century revolution against the federal government which resulted in a whites-only society. Turner's diary entries include instructions on how to build and maintain underground terrorist cells and make a truck bomb. It also chronicles events in the revolution, such as the blowing up of the FBI headquarters in Washington, D.C., and Turner's suicide nuclear attack on the Pentagon. Timothy McVeigh was a big fan of* The Turner Diaries *and tried to persuade his friends and acquaintances to read the book. Photocopies from* The Turner Diaries *were found in McVeigh's car when he was arrested shortly after the bombing. The following description of the bombing of the FBI headquarters from* The Turner Diaries *is strikingly similar to the bombing of the Alfred P. Murrah Federal Building in Oklahoma City.*

October 13, 1991. At 9:15 yesterday morning our bomb went off in the FBI's national headquarters building. Our worries about the relatively small size of the bomb were unfounded; the damage is immense. . . .

The scene in the courtyard was one of utter devastation. The whole Pennsylvania Avenue wing of the building, as we could then see, had collapsed, partly into the courtyard in the center of the building and partly into Pennsylvania Avenue. A huge, gaping hole yawned in the courtyard pave-

near Iraqi government buildings, yet they still proceed with their plans to bomb—saying that they cannot be held responsible if children die. There is no such proof, however, that knowledge of the presence of children existed in relation to the Oklahoma City bombing.)

When considering morality and mens rea [criminal intent] in light of these facts, I ask: Who are the true barbarians?

Yet another example of this nation's blatant hypocrisy is

---

ment just beyond the rubble of collapsed masonry, and it was from this hole that most of the column of black smoke was ascending.

Overturned trucks and automobiles, smashed office furniture, and building rubble were strewn wildly about—and so were the bodies of a shockingly large number of victims. Over everything hung the pall of black smoke, burning our eyes and lungs and reducing the bright morning to semi-darkness. . . .

According to the latest estimate released, approximately 700 persons were killed in the blast or subsequently died in the wreckage. That includes an estimated 150 persons who were in the sub-basement at the time of the explosion and whose bodies have not been recovered.

It may be more than two weeks before enough rubble has been cleared away to allow full access to that level of the building, according to the TV news reporter. . . .

All day yesterday and most of today we watched the TV coverage of rescue crews bringing the dead and injured out of the building. It is a heavy burden of responsibility for us to bear, since most of the victims of our bomb were only pawns who were no more committed to the sick philosophy or the racially destructive goals of the System than we are.

But there is no way we can destroy the System without hurting many thousands of innocent people—no way. It is a cancer too deeply rooted in our flesh. And if we don't destroy the System before it destroys us—if we don't cut this cancer out of our living flesh—our whole race will die.

Andrew MacDonald, *The Turner Diaries*, 1978.

revealed by the polls which suggest that this nation is greatly in favor of bombing Iraq.

In this instance, the people of the nation approve of bombing government employees because they are "guilty by association"—they are Iraqi government employees. In regard to the bombing in Oklahoma City, however, such logic is condemned.

What motivates these seemingly contradictory positions? Do people think that government workers in Iraq are any less human than those in Oklahoma City? Do they think that Iraqis don't have families who will grieve and mourn the loss of their loved ones? In this context, do people come to believe that the killing of foreigners is somehow different than the killing of Americans?

I recently read of an arrest in New York City where possession of a mere pipe bomb was charged as possession of a "weapon of mass destruction." If a two pound pipe bomb is a "weapon of mass destruction," then what do people think that a 2,000-pound steel-encased bomb is?

I find it ironic, to say the least, that one of the aircraft that could be used to drop such a bomb on Iraq is dubbed "The Spirit of Oklahoma."

When a U.S. plane or cruise missile is used to bring destruction to a foreign people, this nation rewards the bombers with applause and praise. What a convenient way to absolve these killers of any responsibility for the destruction they leave in their wake.

Unfortunately, the morality of killing is not so superficial. The truth is, the use of a truck, a plane, or a missile for the delivery of a weapon of mass destruction does not alter the nature of the act itself.

These are weapons of mass destruction—and the method of delivery matters little to those on the receiving end of such weapons.

Whether you wish to admit it or not, when you approve, morally, of the bombing of foreign targets by the U.S. military, you are approving of acts morally equivalent to the bombing in Oklahoma City. The only difference is that this nation is not going to see any foreign casualties appear on the cover of *Newsweek* magazine.

It seems ironic and hypocritical that an act viciously condemned in Oklahoma City is now a "justified" response to a problem in a foreign land. Then again, the history of United States policy over the last century, when examined fully, tends to exemplify hypocrisy.

When considering the use of weapons of mass destruction against Iraq as a means to an end, it would be wise to reflect on the words of the late U.S. Supreme Court Justice Louis Brandeis. His words are as true in the context of Olmstead as they are when they stand alone: "Our government is the potent, the omnipresent teacher. For good or for ill, it teaches the whole people by its example."

Sincerely, Timothy J. McVeigh

Chapter 5

The Trial and Execution

Chapter Preface

Timothy McVeigh and Terry Nichols were indicted on August 10, 1995, by a federal grand jury on eleven counts of conspiracy and murder. In February 1996 U.S. District Court judge Richard Matsch ordered that their trial would be held in Denver, Colorado, because intensive media coverage in Oklahoma had "demonized" the two men to the extent that they would not be able to receive a fair trial anywhere in Oklahoma. Defense lawyers for McVeigh and Nichols argued that in order to provide a fair trial for the two defendants, they should be tried separately since each defendant's strategy would be to blame the other suspect. Matsch agreed and ruled in October 1996 that McVeigh would be tried first.

Jury selection for McVeigh's trial began on March 31, 1997. The prosecution and defense gave their opening statements on April 24. Nearly a month later, and after 137 witnesses had been called to testify, the prosecution rested its case on May 21. The defense took only three and a half days to call 25 witnesses. Both sides gave their closing arguments on May 29, and the jury began its deliberations the next day. McVeigh was convicted on all eleven counts on June 2.

The sentencing phase was next, in which the lawyers presented witnesses to argue for and against the death penalty for McVeigh. The jury unanimously chose the death penalty.

Terry Nichols's trial began on September 29; three months later, the jury found him guilty of conspiracy to use a weapon of mass destruction and involuntary manslaughter for the deaths of eight federal workers. He was found not guilty of two charges: using a weapon of mass destruction and destruction by explosive. He was sentenced to life in prison.

McVeigh's lawyers filed several appeals challenging his conviction and sentence, but eventually McVeigh ordered his lawyers to end the appeals process. On January 16, 2001, Matsch set an execution date of May 16 for McVeigh. On May 11, just five days before McVeigh's scheduled execution, U.S. Attorney General John Ashcroft announced that the FBI had found more than three thousand pages of evidence that had not been turned over to McVeigh's lawyers prior to his trial. Ashcroft delayed McVeigh's execution for thirty days to give his lawyers a chance to look over the material, but Ashcroft contended that there was nothing in the new evidence that would have resulted in a "not guilty" verdict.

On June 1 McVeigh told his lawyers to ask for a stay of execution, but when his request was denied a week later, McVeigh dropped all his other appeals and said he was ready to die. He was executed on June 11, 2001, by lethal injection at the federal prison in Terre Haute, Indiana, without speaking a word to any of the witnesses who came to watch him die. He was pronounced dead at 7:14 A.M.

Finding Probable Cause

Jon Hersley, questioned by Merrick Garland

The first step in Timothy McVeigh's trial was a preliminary hearing held on April 27, 1995, to determine if the prosecution had enough evidence to support its contention that Timothy McVeigh bombed the Murrah federal building. If, at the conclusion of the hearing, the judge determined there was probable cause to believe that McVeigh was the bomber, the charge would be sent to the grand jury who could then issue an indictment against the accused.

The first witness called by the prosecution in McVeigh's preliminary hearing was Jon Hersley, an agent for the FBI. Hersley was questioned by Merrick Garland, the associate deputy attorney general with the U.S. Attorney's office in Oklahoma City. In the following testimony from the hearing, Hersley recounts how the FBI found pieces of the Ryder van that was used in the bombing, traced the truck to its rental agency, and finally, determined who rented it. The FBI also discovered that McVeigh had rented a hotel room—under his own name—in the same city in which the Ryder truck had been rented. McVeigh was also arrested in his car by police about an hour-and-a-half after the bombing, at a location approximately one-and-a-half hours away from Oklahoma City, and analysis of his clothing found trace amounts of explosive residue on them.

Jon Hersley, testimony, *USA v. Timothy James McVeigh*, M-95-98-H, preliminary hearing, April 27, 1995.

Q. State your full name and spell your last name.
A. Jon Hersley, H-E-R-S-L-E-Y.

Q. What is your occupation?

A. I'm an FBI agent.

Q. How long have you been an FBI agent?

A. About 20 years.

Q. Where were you assigned?

A. To the Oklahoma City office of the FBI.

Q. Have you had responsibilities in connection with the investigation of the explosion of the Murrah Building?

A. Yes.

Q. In the course of that investigation, have you spoken with other investigating agents and experts?

A. Yes, I have.

Q. Tell us what happened on April 19, 1995 at the Murrah Building.

A. A bomb exploded at that building, severely damaging the building and causing numerous deaths and injuries.

Q. Approximately what time did the explosion occur?

A. Approximately 9:03 A.M.

The Killed and Injured

Q. Approximately how many people were killed, as far as you know at this time?

A. Approximately 100. I believe it is 101 as of now.

Q. What categories are the people who were killed?

A. That includes numerous Federal employees; I believe there were 15 children that were killed at this point whose bodies have been found, and there were also several Federal law enforcement officers that were killed in the bombing.

Q. Are there any people still missing?

A. Yes.

Q. How many?

A. Between 100 and 150 is what I have heard.

Q. Do you know how many people were injured, approximately?

A. Approximately 400.

Q. What is the Murrah Building used for?

A. It houses numerous Federal agencies, Federal employees that work there.

Q. Is it used by agencies of the United States?

A. Yes, it is.

Q. Would you describe some of those agencies?

A. The U.S. Drug Enforcement Administration, the Bureau of Alcohol, Tobacco and Firearms, the U.S. Secret Service, Department of Housing and Urban Development, the Social Security Administration, and numerous other Federal agencies.

The Bomb

Q. Have you consulted with explosive experts of the FBI?

A. Yes.

Q. What caused the explosion of the Murrah Building?

A. A bomb.

Q. Have the experts informed you as to where the bomb was located at the time it went off?

A. Yes.

Q. Please describe that to the Court.

A. It was located inside a Ryder Truck that was parked in front of the Murrah Building on the north side.

Q. How did the experts know that?

A. Due to the uniqueness of the blast damage that was suffered on certain components of the truck, they are able to tell that it was actually located inside that truck.

Q. Has an effort been made to trace that Ryder Truck to the point of which it was rented?

A. Yes.

The Ryder Truck

Q. What methods are used to trace that truck?

A. There was a portion of the vehicle identification number that was located and we were able to trace from that portion the full vehicle identification number and then take that on to determine who actually had the vehicle.

Q. In addition to the vehicle identification number, or

VIN number, was there another part of the truck that permitted tracing?

A. Yes.

Q. What was that?

A. The license plate.

Q. I have marked what will be called Government's Exhibit 1 for identification and I am showing it to defense counsel.

Do you recognize Government's Exhibit 1?

A. Yes, I do.

Q. What is Government's Exhibit 1?

A. This is the Florida license plate that was on the Ryder Truck. . . .

Q. You said that by using the vehicle identification number and the license plate, that you were able to trace the truck to a rental location; is that correct?

A. Yes.

Q. What was the result of that tracing?

A. The Elliott's Body Shop in Junction City, Kansas.

Q. Was the rental agent at that location interviewed?

A. Yes.

Q. Did he advise as to when that truck was rented?

A. Yes.

Q. When was that?

A. The truck was rented on April 17th of this year.

Q. By how many people?

A. One person filled out the rental agreement; there was another individual with that person when they picked it up.

Identifying the Bomber

Q. What did the individual who filled out the rental agreement provide on the rental agreement?

A. Provided his name.

Q. Did he provide any other identifying information?

A. Yes, I believe a Social Security account number, as well as a driver's license and also his address.

Q. Was an effort made to trace the Social Security number or driver's license and address?

A. Yes.

Q. What was the result of that tracing?

A. They were both his numbers.

Q. Did the rental agent assist in the creation of a composite drawing of the individual who rented the truck?

A. Yes.

MR. GARLAND: Your Honor, I have what has been marked as Government's Exhibit 2 for identification.

(Government's counsel displays Exhibit 2 to counsel.)

Q. Do you recognize Government's Exhibit 2?

A. Yes, I do.

Q. What is Government's Exhibit 2?

A. This is the composite drawing that was prepared.

Q. It was prepared with the information provided by who?

A. By the employee at the Elliott's Body Shop.

Q. Did he advise the FBI as to whether that composite drawing was a fair and accurate representation of the person that rented the truck?

A. Yes, he said it was. . . .

MR. GARLAND: I ask the Court to take its own notice as to its resemblance to the Defendant.

The Dreamland Hotel

Q. (By Mr. Garland) Mr. Hersley, is there also a hotel named the Dreamland Hotel in Junction City, Kansas?

A. Yes.

Q. Had interviewing been done at that hotel?

A. Yes.

Q. What did people at the hotel advise the agents?

A. That an individual had checked into the hotel on April 14th of this year.

Q. How long did he stay?

A. Until April 18th.

Q. Was any connection made between the individual and the representation in Exhibit 2?

A. Yes.

Q. What was that connection?

A. The individual at the hotel advised that the individual

that had stayed at the Dreamland Hotel between April 14th and April 18th of this year strongly resembled the composite picture.

Q. What name did he register under at the hotel?

A. Tim McVeigh.

Q. Did he provide an address?

A. Yes.

Q. What was that address?

A. 3616 North Van Dyke in Decker, Michigan.

Q. Was he seen driving any automobile at the time?

A. Yes.

Q. What kind of automobile?

A. A yellow Mercury.

Room 25

Q. What room did he register in at the hotel?

A. Room 25.

Q. Were the employees at the Dreamland—were any employees at the Dreamland shown a photo spread which included a picture of Mr. McVeigh?

A. Yes.

Q. What was the result of that photo identification?

A. The employee positively identified the picture depicting Timothy McVeigh as being the person that stayed at the room on that occasion.

Q. What was that room?

A. Room 25.

Q. Was an analysis made of telephone calls from the Dreamland Motel during that period?

A. Yes.

Q. Was there a call on April 15th—

A. Yes.

Q.—from Room 25?

A. Yes, there was.

Q. Is that the same room that Mr. McVeigh was registered in?

A. That's correct.

Q. Where was that call made to?

A. To a local restaurant in Junction City.

Q. Have you examined the receipt of the restaurant for that date?

A. Yes.

Q. What does it show?

A. It shows that the order was placed by an individual using the name "Kling."

Q. Is "Kling" the same name as on the Ryder Truck form?

A. Yes.

Q. Did it show what room number the order came from?

A. Yes, Room 25.

Q. Was a photo spread shown to the delivery man?

A. Yes.

Q. Was he able to identify Mr. McVeigh?

A. No.

Q. On April 17th, that was the day that the Ryder Truck was rented; is that correct?

A. That's correct.

Eyewitnesses

Q. Did any Dreamland employee see Mr. McVeigh?

A. Yes.

Q. In what connection did they see him?

A. They saw him arrive at the Dreamland Motel driving the Ryder Truck.

Q. On April 18, the following day, did any employee of the Dreamland Motel see Mr. McVeigh?

A. Yes.

Q. How did they see him then?

A. At approximately 4 A.M., Mr. McVeigh was observed in the Ryder Truck.

Q. Later in the day did they again see Mr. McVeigh in the Ryder Truck?

A. No.

Q. Now, in Paragraph 6 of the Affidavit that was attached to the Complaint in this case there is a discussion of three witnesses who identified a person in Exhibit 2, the composite, as having been in the vicinity of the Murrah Building on the morning of the explosion; is that correct?

A. Yes, it is.

Q. Have those people been able to confirm that they saw the Defendant, Tim McVeigh?

A. No.

Q. On April 19th, is that the date of the bomb?

A. Yes.

Q. Was Mr. McVeigh arrested on that day?

A. Yes, he was.

The Arrest

Q. Would you explain that, please.

A. At approximately 10:30 A.M., Mr. McVeigh was arrested by an Oklahoma Highway Patrol Trooper at a location near Perry, Oklahoma.

Q. The reason for the stop?

A. Mr. McVeigh's yellow Mercury did not have a license plate on it at that time and he was stopped for that reason.

Q. About what time was the stop?

A. Approximately 10:30 A.M.

Q. About how long after the blast was that?

A. Approximately one-and-a-half hours.

Q. Where was the stop?

A. Near Perry, Oklahoma.

Q. Approximately how long of a drive is it from the Murrah Building to Perry, Oklahoma?

A. Less than an hour-and-a-half.

Q. I want to show you what has been marked as Government's Exhibit 3 for identification.

(Government's counsel displays Exhibit 3 to counsel.)

Q. (By Mr. Garland) Do you recognize Government's Exhibit 3?

A. Yes, I do.

Q. What is Government's Exhibit 3?

A. It is a Michigan driver's license in the name of Timothy James McVeigh.

Q. Where was it obtained?

A. From Mr. McVeigh.

Q. At the time of the arrest?

A. Yes.

Q. Does it show an address?

A. Yes.

Q. What is that?

A. 3616 North Van Dyke Road, Decker, Michigan.

Q. Is that the same street and town as the entry on the Dreamland Motel register?

A. Yes, it is.

More Evidence

Q. When Mr. McVeigh was stopped, was anything found on his person?

A. Yes.

Q. What was that?

A. He had a Glock .45 semi-automatic in a shoulder holster, with two magazines.

Q. Was the Glock loaded?

A. Yes.

Q. What kind of bullets did it contain?

A. Black talon.

Q. Is there a street name for the black talon bullet?

A. Yes.

Q. What is that name?

A. It is referred to as a "cop-killer bullet."

Q. Was Mr. McVeigh's clothing tested?

A. Yes.

Q. What was the results of the test?

A. It tested positive for traces of PETN.

Q. What is PETN?

A. Penta erythratol tetral nitrate.

Q. What is penta erythratol tetral nitrate?

A. It is an explosive that is commonly used in detonating cord.

MR. GARLAND: The Government has no further questions.

A Pack of Lies

Stephen Jones

Timothy McVeigh's trial on murder, conspiracy, and weapons charges did not begin until more than two years after the bombing in Oklahoma City. Due to the massive publicity surrounding the case in Oklahoma City, the judge hearing the case ruled that McVeigh could not receive a fair trial anywhere in Oklahoma and so moved it to Denver, Colorado. McVeigh chose to exercise his right to be tried by a jury of his peers. The trial officially opened with opening arguments by the prosecuting and defense attorneys. Since the government had the burden of proving the charges, it presented its argument first, followed by the defense's opening statement. Opening arguments are not evidence, but simply summarize the facts of the case that each side expects will be presented during testimony.

Timothy McVeigh's legal team consisted of dozens of lawyers—all paid by the U.S. government since McVeigh was considered indigent. McVeigh's lead attorney was Stephen Jones, who had represented several high-profile defendants and accused murderers in more than a dozen death-penalty cases prior to his being assigned to McVeigh's case. In his opening statement to the jury, Jones contended that an important witness for the prosecution—Michael Fortier—was lying about what he knew about the bombing. Fortier maintained for weeks that McVeigh was innocent of the crime, even going so far as to hold press conferences announcing his belief in his friend's innocence. Jones asserts that when an accomplice—Terry Nichols—was arrested in connection with the bombing, Fortier realized he, too, could be arrested for the crime, and so Fortier agreed to testify for the prosecution

Stephen Jones, opening statement, *USA v. Timothy James McVeigh*, Criminal Action No. 96-CR-68, April 24, 1997.

in exchange for a reduced sentence. Jones contends that everything Fortier told the prosecution about McVeigh's actions concerning the bombing could have been discovered simply by following the news. Fortier changed his story and lied to protect himself, Jones alleges.

I t was a spring day in Oklahoma City. And inside the office of the Social Security Administration located in the Alfred P. Murrah Building, named after a distinguished chief judge of the United States Court of Appeals for the Tenth Circuit, a young black woman named Daina Bradley was feeling the atmosphere a little stuffy and warm; so she left her mother, her two children, and her sister in line and she wandered out into the lobby of the Alfred P. Murrah Building. And as she was looking out the plate glass window, a Ryder truck slowly pulled into a parking place and stopped. She didn't give it any particular attention until the door opened on the passenger side, and she saw a man get out.

The Description Does Not Match

Approximately three weeks later, she described the man to the Federal Bureau of Investigation agents, as indeed she did to us and to others, as short, stocky, olive-complected, wearing a puffy jacket, with black hair, a description that does not match my client. She did not see anyone else. She saw this individual pause briefly, walk to what she thought might be the back of the truck, and walk away. She turned around and went back in the Social Security office; and then in just a matter of moments, the explosion occurred. It took the life of her mother and her two children and horribly burned her sister. She is not a witness for the defense.

And that night, approximately 12 hours later, almost to the minute, somewhere between 50 and 100 million people throughout the world, courtesy of CNN, watched physicians crawl through the rubble of the Murrah Building and amputate this woman's life—this woman's leg in order that her life might be saved and she could be extricated from the rubble. . . .

Not the Right Man

In reviewing the evidence in this case and in the proof that will come, you know, and certainly it will be in evidence, that this was the largest domestic terrorism act in the history of this country. The president of the United States and the Attorney General of the United States went on nationwide television within hours after the bombing. The president came to Oklahoma City for the memorial funeral service at which 12,000 people attended. The federal government offered a $2 million reward for information leading to the arrest and conviction of those involved. And I think it fair to say that this was the largest criminal investigation in the history of this country. The question is did they get the right man. . . .

I believe that when you see the evidence in this case, you will conclude that the investigation of the Alfred P. Murrah Building lasted about two weeks. The investigation to build the case against Timothy McVeigh lasted about two years. But within 72 hours after suspicion first centered on Mr. McVeigh, we will prove to you that even then, the Government knew, the FBI agents in the case, that the pieces of the puzzle were not coming together; that there was something terribly wrong, something missing. And as Paul Harvey says, our evidence will be the rest of the story. So let me begin first with Timothy McVeigh. . . .

Who Is Timothy McVeigh?

He came to Arizona [in 1993], where his friends Mike and Lori Fortier lived; and Tim worked at the TruValue Hardware store in Kingman beginning in 1993 and again as a security guard at State Security during the same period of time. And then he went to work, so to speak, on his own, buying and selling and trading weapons at the numerous gun shows held throughout the country, of which there are probably anywhere from 2- to 3,000 a year. . . .

Mr. McVeigh's motives as described by the Government in Mr. Hartzler's opening address are that he is anti-government; that he has a hatred for the United States, and that he conspired with others to build a terrible explosive de-

vice which he initiated because he was angry at the government of the United States. . . .

His politics were open and known to everyone that spent
any time with him. There was no secret about the politics
that Tim McVeigh had.

Waco

And part of those politics had to do with the events . . . at
Waco and Ruby Ridge [two distinct events in which government officers killed civilians who defied government
policies]. Our proof will be that Tim McVeigh believed that
the federal government executed 76 people at Waco, including 30 women and 25 children. That was his political
belief. He was not alone in that opinion.

He believed that the federal law enforcement at Waco de-
ployed in a military fashion against American citizens and
children who had committed no crime and that the Branch
Davidians were not a cult who lived in a compound. He believed that they were what they were, a breakoff of the Seventh Day Adventist church who had lived at Mount Carmel
since the 1930's.

He believed that the federal government undertook a
course of action including the use of tanks and CS gas and
other military weapons against the Branch Davidians which
was certain to result in their death. He believed that federal
agents fired upon the Davidians as they attempted to escape
the fire. He believed that these actions and cover-up of these
actions, as he saw it, pointed to a federal government out of
control; and he made no secret about it. He was at Waco.
There is a videotape of Tim McVeigh which you will see in
evidence in a flannel shirt sitting on top of his car, talking
to a television reporter. And on the top of the car are bumper
stickers that he is selling or giving away which describe his
political beliefs.

He believed that the government manipulated the press at
Waco and that the words "cult" and "compound" were used
to hide what was really going on.

He was not alone in those beliefs. When the federal jury

at San Antonio acquitted the Branch Davidians of murder, he saw that as validation; and when the Congress of the United States last year issued its report on Waco, he saw that as validation.

He was also concerned about Ruby Ridge, where Marshal Deacon, much celebrated member of the United States Marshal's Service, was killed. He believed there that the ATF had entrapped Randy Weaver into committing a crime by sawing off a small portion of a shotgun just below the line to make it illegal so that they could then pressure Weaver into being an informant for the ATF in the community in northern Idaho 20 miles from the Canadian border that Weaver had moved his family to, to live life as he wanted. . . .

Ruby Ridge acquitted Randy Weaver of murder. So his views weren't alone, and they certainly were not secret. . . .

The federal government's actions in reference to . . . Waco trigger emotional responses from people like Tim McVeigh; but they are within the political and social mainstream. And among those people who held the same views were Michael and Lori Fortier. Each of them expressed frequently the same views ascribed to Tim McVeigh. We will show you evidence that Michael Fortier himself believed that the Government had murdered innocent children at Waco and had used excessive force at Ruby Ridge. The evidence of Michael and Lori Fortier will show that people can have deep-seated convictions about these matters without being prompted to action. . . .

The Prosecution Needs the Fortiers

[Prosecuting attorney Mr. Joseph] Hartzler told you that he would call as witnesses to offer evidence Michael and Lori Fortier. He told you, "We could prove the case without them," that they are certainly not dependent upon them. Here is what the proof will show: They cannot prove the case without Michael Fortier; for under the evidence we will present, if they could, they would have charged Michael Fortier.

The proof will also show—and Mr. Hartzler alluded to it—that Mr. Fortier has pled guilty but he has not yet been sentenced. His wife received a form of immunity, which he described for you, so she cannot be prosecuted at all. The proof is that under the Government's theory, either one of these individuals, if what they say is true, could have stopped this bombing. They did not.

The proof will also show that at the conclusion of this case, Mr. Fortier at some time will be sentenced; and part of his plea bargain is that the Government may move for a downward departure of his sentencing guidelines. What those are will be explained by witnesses, but basically they will show that Mr. Fortier could face up to 23 years in prison or he could be sentenced to as little as two years in prison. . . .

They Knew the Government's Theories

Michael and Lori Fortier's political beliefs were very similar to Tim McVeigh's. That's one of the reasons for their friendship. They were completely aware of Mr. McVeigh's government theories, and they were also completely aware— and we will introduce evidence to that effect—of the Government's theory in this case about Tim McVeigh long before they made any statements to the FBI concerning that theory. In other words, the proof will show that what they told the Government they had already read about in the *Kingman Daily Miner* and the *Arizona Republic* and seen on television and probably heard on the radio what the Government's theory was. Beginning on April the 19, 1995, and continuing for almost a full month until May 17, 1995, the Fortiers read countless newspaper articles, watched constant television coverage concerning the Government's investigation of the Oklahoma City bombing. They will admit to you that they studied these news accounts before making any statements which would tend to support the Government's theory.

Aspects of the Government's case which we will introduce which appeared prominently in the newspapers and media sources directly available to the Fortiers include the following: That the Government believed that the bomb was carried in a Ryder truck; that the Government believed the truck was rented at Elliott's Body Shop in Junction City,

Kansas; that the person that rented the truck had used the alias Robert Kling; that the Government believed the bomb was constructed at Geary Lake State Park; that the Government believed Tim McVeigh left a getaway car in Oklahoma City on April 16, 1995; that the Government believed that Terry Nichols and Tim McVeigh had constructed the bomb and that Tim McVeigh had driven the truck which carried the bomb; that the Government believed that storage sheds were used to conceal the components of the bomb; and that the Government believed the bomb was constructed of ammonium nitrate and fuel oil contained within plastic barrels.

All of that Michael Fortier knew was the Government's theory before he began cooperating with the Government. Not only did they read these accounts in the *Arizona Republic* newspaper, they had access to the *Kingman Daily Miner*, their hometown newspaper, which was full of details concerning it because the FBI was conducting a wide-ranging investigation in Kingman.

The proof will show that Michael and Lori Fortier's subsequent statements were designed to support the reports that they had read about . . . the Government's theory before they decided to cooperate.

Vehement Denials

In fact, Michael Fortier would admit to you that he went so far as to confront the FBI with a copy of the *Arizona Republic* newspaper of Sunday, April 23, 1995, concerning what he said were false reports. Notations and highlights that Mr. Fortier set forth in the newspaper itself, include "never knew him to shoot illegally," "not true to my knowledge," "anyone charged not convicted should fear for their lives," "guilty until proven innocent."

In reference to Mr. Nichols frequenting Mr. Fortier's home, Mr. Fortier wrote, "Never, ever, pure fabrication, which will be taken as true," and quote, "Never heard of this story," close quote.

So the evidence will clearly show that he followed the Government's investigation and knew what they were doing from the newspaper. The evidence will show that these reports that he read, which he now supports, before he began to cooperate with the Government, he vehemently denied to the FBI, to friends, to CNN, *Los Angeles Times* and anybody else that talked with him.

The Government will offer evidence and proof, we believe, that Mr. Fortier visited various sites associated with this case under the Government's theory. But our evidence is that Michael Fortier knew these sites. He had lived in Junction City, Kansas. He had been at Fort Riley. He had been through Herington. He knew where Geary State Lake was. He knew all of this area because he and Lori had lived there during the time that he was in the military. He had been stationed at Fort Riley for three years and lived in Manhattan, Kansas, right in the center of this area, for two of those years. He had also traveled through Oklahoma City with Tim McVeigh when both of them were in the service in 1988. But in addition to his military service, the evidence will show that both Michael and Lori Fortier had the same political philosophy attributed to Tim McVeigh and, incidentally, Terry Nichols. Both Michael and Lori were outraged over the Government's actions at Waco, and Michael Fortier told the FBI as much. Both possessed and used firearms, and Michael Fortier possessed explosives; and they possessed all of the same literature or certainly much of it that was found in a box that one of Jennifer's friends was keeping of Tim McVeigh's belongings. Michael Fortier possessed a copy of what's called *The Citizens' Rule Book*. He was a subscriber to the *Spotlight* newsletter just like my client and a subscriber to the *Patriot Reports*, and he possessed his own copy of *The Turner Diaries*.

Proclaiming Tim's Innocence

Michael and Lori Fortier, we will prove, proclaimed Tim McVeigh's innocence to the world repeatedly. They even prepared a written press release that Lori Fortier wrote out which Michael Fortier delivered in an interview with Sean Calebs of CNN on April the 26th, 1995.

Beginning on April the 21st, the proof will show, Mr. Fortier made seven separate detailed statements to the FBI in which he denied knowledge of the bombing and proclaimed Tim's innocence. Lori Fortier was present for most if not all of these statements.

Even after Mr. Fortier began cooperating with the FBI on May 17, 1995, he claimed that he did not know the guns provided by McVeigh had been stolen in this robbery that the Government will introduce evidence concerning; and Mr. Fortier at that time made no mention of the Marion County quarry burglary that Mr. Hartzler mentioned to you. But after he had numerous contacts—and there will be proof of those—with agents, then Mr. Fortier remembered those details and added to them.

The Government obtained court-ordered surveillance by electronic means of Mr. and Mrs. Fortier. They followed them when they left their apartment. They made their presence well known. They kept surveillance logs—you'll see them—and were following them almost heel to toe. But they followed them in a way that the Fortiers did not know because they had made, as the law permits, an application to the district court out there to obtain what we call a bug, placing it inside the Fortiers' house so that every word Michael and Lori said was secretly recorded without their knowledge. And in addition, they had a tap on the telephone so that whoever called—and most of the phone calls were from media sources seeking interviews—but whoever called, their father, their mother, their friends, their brother, those conversations, unbeknownst to the Fortiers, were secretly tape-recorded; and you will hear some of them.

"No Knowledge"

On April the 21st, Mr. Fortier was questioned by the FBI; and he stated to them that he knew that Mr. McVeigh had been charged because of TV coverage, but he told the FBI that he did not think Tim McVeigh was capable of participation in the Oklahoma City bombing.

He was interviewed a second time on the same day by the

FBI, and this time he told the FBI that he had not seen or had contact with Terry Nichols since Mr. Fortier was discharged from the Army. He also told them that he had no knowledge of or complicity in the bombing.

The next day, April 22nd, Mr. Fortier told FBI agents that the Oklahoma City investigation was a witch hunt, and he stated unequivocally that he did not believe McVeigh did it. The following day he was reinterviewed, and Mr. Fortier told the FBI that Mr. McVeigh had never spoken generally or specifically about any bombs; and it was Mr. Fortier that said that he had not cried over the children killed in Oklahoma City because children are being killed all over the world.

In a second interview on April the 23rd, 1985 (sic), Mr. Fortier told agents that he had never been involved with explosives and only discussed guns with the Government—and the Government with Tim McVeigh. He again told the FBI that he picked up no indication whatsoever from Tim McVeigh that Mr. McVeigh would commit the Oklahoma City bombing. The next day he was again interviewed; and on April 24th, he again told the FBI, "I have no knowledge of the bombing."

The Search Warrant

On May the 1st, the FBI warned Mr. Fortier they were going to search his house, they had obtained a search warrant. The evidence will show that ordinarily search warrants are executed and carried out without calling somebody on the phone or telling them they're going to be searched, because of course they might hide or destroy evidence. You get the search warrant, you go out and search somebody's house. Our proof is this: The Government knew that Mr. Fortier had drugs, he used them, maybe distributed them, possessed them. They didn't want to find drugs in his house, so they told him they were going to search it. Mr. Fortier took the drugs out, gave them to his next-door neighbor, and there were no drugs there when the FBI arrived a few minutes later.

On May the 6th, Mr. Fortier was served with a grand jury subpoena, and he told the agents he didn't think he could be of any additional help because he didn't know anything; and then a few days later—and there will be evidence on this—something happened. On Wednesday, May 10th, an article appeared in the *Phoenix Gazette* which indicated that Terry Nichols had now been charged as a direct participant in the Oklahoma City bombing. Mr. Fortier read this article, and he now understood that Mr. Nichols as well as Mr. McVeigh could face the death penalty if convicted. He also understood from the article that Mr. Nichols was being charged not only as a direct participant but as an aider and abettor of the crime. The article he read indicated that Mr. Nichols and Mr. McVeigh had a long association, just like Mr. Fortier and Mr. McVeigh had; that Mr. Nichols and Mr. McVeigh had been through basic training together. And Mr. Fortier will tell you he had been through basic training with them; that they had sometimes shared a house together. Mr. Fortier will tell you that he and Mr. McVeigh had shared a house together. The article indicated that the FBI and authorities had found guns, ammunition, antigovernment literature and other material at Terry Nichols' house.

Mr. Fortier will tell you that he had guns and ammunition, explosives and antigovernment literature at his house. He perceived he would be next, our proof is. He had a long association with Tim just like Terry. Like Mr. Nichols, Mr. McVeigh and Fortier had gone through basic training together, they both shared a house together, they both had fertilizer at their houses; and like Nichols, Mr. Fortier had guns, ammunition and antigovernment literature.

Public and Private Statements

Two days after Terry Nichols had been charged as a participant in the Oklahoma City bombing, on May 12, 1995, Michael Fortier contacted the FBI and told them he wanted to cooperate. Prior to this meeting with the FBI at which he had wanted to cooperate, in the sanctity of his own home, Mr. Fortier told, through these wiretaps and bugs, his closest friends and his family that he had no knowledge of the bombing and that Tim McVeigh was innocent.

In the privacy of his home and on the privacy of his telephone away from the television and newspaper and FBI agents outside, he specifically stated the following: He told his brother John that the FBI played games, lied to him and used intimidation against him and his wife. He told his brother John that the FBI implied that they were going to change the sketch of John Doe 2 to make it look like Fortier, and he repeated those concerns in a nationwide interview on CNN. He told his brother John that the FBI had planted earplugs in his Jeep. He told his friend Lonnie Hubbard that "The FBI harassed the fuck out of me." He told Lonnie Hubbard that, quote, "I don't know jack," close quote, about the Oklahoma City bombing.

He told his father that he had been truthful to the FBI when he said he had no knowledge, and he told his father that he didn't believe Tim would ever do anything like the Oklahoma City bombing. He told his mother and his brother, Irene Fortier and Paul Fortier, that the FBI had been lying to his family; and he then said, "All I know is they don't tell you the truth."

"Tim Is Not Responsible"

But he didn't just make these statements to his family in the privacy of his home. He repeated them publicly. I've already mentioned the handwritten press release. And in the statement, Michael and Lori Fortier say the following:

> I would also like to say to everyone that Timothy McVeigh is a close friend of my family and mine. He stands accused of the bombing of the Alfred P. Murrah Building; but from knowing him, I believe in no way he was responsible for this crime. This country has been a witness to how the alleged suspect, Timothy McVeigh, has already been crucified by all the lies put forth by the media. We have all seen how the alleged suspect, Timothy McVeigh, has been portrayed in the media; and it truly sickens me when I see my friend's—yes, my friend's—face portrayed on the front of *Time* magazine as the face of terror. All of this for what reason? Premise was he was arrested and charged in connection with the bombing of the Alfred P. Murrah Building. It was only because he fit the description of a composite sketch. In this country

there are probably a half a million people that could fit that sketch. Hell, for that matter, there are probably a lot of people who fit it better than Tim. What I mean by this is Tim's actual physical description is 6'2" to 6'3", 160 to 165 pounds, male, far from the composite sketch of John Doe 1's description of a 5'8" to 5'11", 180- to 185-pound male. They better have more than this to arrest the man; but then again, they needed somebody to arrest for this crime.

That's what he said. The proof will show that on April the 27, 1995, Mr. and Mrs. Fortier at their own initiative traveled to a park near their home for the purpose of an interview with CNN. He gave a detailed interview to the reporter, and he said the following, in part:

> I have spoken with the FBI, and I get the impression that sketch is being modif[ied] to fit my face. I mean that I know my friend Tim McVeigh is not the face of terror reported on *Time* magazine. I cannot say that. See, everybody just assumes that he did it automatically, and everybody wants to know why he did it or, you know, what he was thinking and stuff like that. The only fact is that this man was caught speeding on a highway in Oklahoma, and that is his only crime; and that why he speeds, I don't know. I'm not sure what you're insinuating what Nichols said; but no, no, I don't believe that Tim blew up any building in Oklahoma. There is nothing for me to look back upon and say, ah, yeah, that might have been. I should have seen it back then. There was nothing like that, you know; and everybody should be supportive of him because he's an innocent man.

Double-Checking Their Stories

From time to time, the proof will show, Michael and Lori Fortier checked and double-checked to be sure that their statements were consistent before they made their first joint statement to the FBI.

On May the 17th, 1995, in a Motel 6 room in Oklahoma City, Michael and Lori Fortier had a one-hour, private meeting to discuss what they would say to the FBI.

We will offer evidence that they have been in constant communication ever since then.

Mr. Hartzler told you that the Fortiers would admit, under the Government's proof, that they were users of amphetamines and marijuana. The proof will be they were daily users of amphetamines during the period of time for which they claim to have knowledge.

Mr. Fortier was a daily seller of amphetamines, both Michael and Lori used marijuana; and the evidence will show, as I've already indicated, that the Government wasn't interested in pursuing that; but Mr. Fortier didn't know that. Mr. Fortier's maximum punishment, under the charges that he pled guilty to, is 23 years but he faces over a hundred years if he had been charged with the other crimes for which he was not charged, multiple counts of drug use and possession and lying to the ATF.

Our proof is that what he could have been charged with that he did is far greater in its severity than that which he pled guilty to but didn't do; and of course, as Mr. Hartzler told you, no charges were filed against his wife whose drug use and habit was almost as great as Mr. Fortier's.

The FBI repeatedly told Mr. Fortier in the interviews that participants in the Oklahoma City bombing would face the death penalty. Our evidence is that Terry Nichols appeared to be in the same circumstantial position by Mr. Fortier and that Mr. Fortier could read the writing on the wall.

The Fortiers' Deal

In the plea negotiations that Mr. Hartzler has referenced the government offered Mr. Fortier a deal which allowed he and his wife to escape death itself. Mr. Fortier believed, and he will tell you, that under the deal he could receive as little as two years and his wife would not be prosecuted at all.

The deal, as I indicated, and you'll see it in evidence, provides that the Government will file a motion for a lower sentence in the event Mr. Fortier, quote, "cooperated," close quote.

The bottom line was, and is, that under this agreement which will be introduced, in order to testify against . . . Mr. McVeigh, Mr. Fortier would avoid a federal prison sentence in excess of 50 years for false statements to the FBI, false statements to the ATF and drug possession and distribution all of which, the proof will show, are totally unrelated to the bombing of the Murrah Building; but in the Oklahoma City bombing case, under the agreement, he escapes capital prosecution and his wife avoids prosecution altogether. Our proof is that under such circumstances Mr. and Mrs. Fortier could only be expected to say whatever the Government wanted to hear, and we will prove they tailored their testimony to fit what they already knew about the prosecution's case and theory and save their own skins at the expense of the truth.

We will prove that Mr. Fortier's testimony against Mr. McVeigh is the product of fear and intimidation, that he proclaimed Mr. McVeigh's innocence to his closest friends and the world and changed when Mr. Terry Nichols was charged. . . .

No Evidence

If Tim McVeigh built the bomb and put it in the truck, our proof will be that his fingernails, his nostrils, his hair, his clothing, his car, his shoes, his socks would have it all over them. They don't.

Out of 7,000 pounds of debris, there is less than half a dozen pieces of evidence of a forensic nature; and we will go over each one of them with you. And our evidence will be that they do not prove Mr. McVeigh guilty or a participant in this bombing.

I apologize for the time—I don't apologize. I take it back. I don't apologize for the time. This is an important case. You know it. It's the only opportunity I will have probably for several weeks, if not several months, before we put on our case. I thank you for your attention, and I believe that you now know what I meant when I said every pancake has two sides.

Thank you.

A Witness to the Plot

Michael Fortier, questioned by Joseph Hartzler

One of the principal witnesses in Timothy McVeigh's trial for bombing the federal building in Oklahoma City was Michael Fortier. Fortier and McVeigh had been good friends for many years; they had served in the army together and McVeigh had been Fortier's best man at his wedding. However, Fortier testified against McVeigh during his trial. Fortier struck a deal with prosecutors; prosecutors would recommend a reduced sentence on unrelated weapons charges in exchange for his testimony about what McVeigh had told him about the plot to bomb the federal building.

The following is an excerpt of Fortier's testimony. Responding to questions by prosecutor Joseph Hartzler, Fortier stated that McVeigh was determined to take offensive action against the government he felt murdered innocent civilians in a raid on the Branch Davidian cult in Waco, Texas. He said McVeigh asked if he would participate in the attack, but Fortier declined. He said McVeigh even drove him to Oklahoma City and showed him which building he was going to bomb and told him other details about the bombing.

After the trial, Fortier was sentenced to a fine of $200,000 and twelve years in prison; he could have been sentenced to as many as twenty-three years.

Q. Mr. Fortier, do you know Timothy McVeigh?
A. Yes, sir, I do.
Q. When and where did you first meet him?
A. In Fort Benning, Georgia, when I entered the service in 1988.

Michael Fortier, testimony, *USA v. Timothy James McVeigh*, Criminal Action No. 96-CR-68, May 12, 1997.

Q. That was the Army?

A. Yes, sir.

Q. And did you become friends with Mr. McVeigh?

A. Yes.

Q. So just calculate for us how long you have known Mr. McVeigh.

A. Nine years. . . .

Q. And did he ever visit you or did you visit him anyplace after you both were discharged from the Army?

A. Tim visited me in Kingman, Arizona.

Q. As best you can recall, tell us when approximately it was that he first visited you in Kingman.

A. Best I can recall, he came to see me in April of 1993.

Discussing Waco

Q. Now, do you recall the tragedy that occurred at the Branch Davidian compound near Waco, Texas?

A. Yes, sir.

Q. And did you follow that event on the news?

A. Yes, I did.

Q. Mr. McVeigh arrived, as you recall, approximately when in relationship to that incident?

A. Just after the fire destroyed the compound.

Q. And do you recall having any discussions with him about that?

A. Yes, sir. . . .

We just discussed the legality of it. We both concluded that the federal government had intentionally attacked those people and maybe not intentionally started the fire, but they were certainly the cause of the fire and potentially they murdered those people in Waco. . . .

McVeigh Plots to Take Action

Q. Do you recall that letter [from McVeigh in August 1994]?

A. Yes, sir.

Q. You read it?

A. Yes, I read it.

Q. Tell us what it said.

A. Tim told me that him and Terry Nichols had decided to take some type of positive offensive action. He wanted to know if I wanted to partake of it; if I did, I would have to keep it a secret from my wife. That's basically what the letter said.

Q. What did you do with the letter?

A. I showed my wife the letter.

Q. Did you respond to that letter?

A. Yes, sir. I told him in my letter that I was curious what he was talking about, but then I would in no way keep any secrets from my wife.

Q. So your response did not reject the idea of taking action; is that fair?

A. I was curious to what he was talking about.

Q. But you invited further conversation at least; you did not reject the idea of taking action against the government; is that a fair characterization?

A. Yes.

Q. After receiving and responding to that letter, did you have further contact with Mr. McVeigh that year?

A. Yes, sir. . . .

Tim was at my house. I don't remember much about this visit. It was real short, just a few days. We had a conversation near my fence in my front yard. Tim was telling me what he meant by taking action. He told me that he—him and Terry were thinking of blowing up a building.

Q. Is that the first time you had heard him discuss using explosives to blow up something?

A. Yes, sir.

Q. Other than obviously the desert experience?

A. Yes.

Q. And did he try to persuade you to participate in this activity?

A. Yes. He asked me to help them. I turned him down. I said I would never do anything like that unless there was— until the time that there was a UN tank in my front yard.

Q. What was your reference to having a UN tank in your front yard?

A. Obviously if there was a UN tank sitting in my front yard, we would be at a state of war with the New World Order, and I feel that actions like that would be appropriate at that time, but not before. . . .

Explosives

Q. Do you recall your next contact with him, after he stopped at your house?

A. Yes.

Q. When was that?

A. It was either that night, or maybe it was a few nights later, he showed up at my house almost at 9:00 on the dot. I remember looking at the clock on my wall and seeing that.

Q. So it was dark outside?

A. Yes, sir.

Q. And was he alone?

A. No, he wasn't. He came at my house and asked me to come with him, he wanted to show me something. I went with him in his car. We followed Terry Nichols in his truck to the storage sheds that are near my house. . . .

Q. And when you got to the storage unit area, what happened?

A. We got into a storage locker that they had rented, and Tim showed me some explosives that were inside it.

Q. Do you recall what explosives you saw?

A. I don't recall exactly the explosives I seen that night. What I recall, Tim had a flashlight, and the main part of the beam was shining on the box; and it had a—and one of those orange triangles or yellow triangles—not a triangle. Excuse me—a diamond that says "explosives." That's what I remember seeing mostly.

Q. And you were actually shown some of these explosives?

A. Tim was reaching into the box and showing me some explosives, but I don't remember exactly what it was he showed me.

Q. And do you recall how much else was in the storage locker?

A. Well, he was squatted down before a blanket that was

covering some items that appeared to be more of the boxes containing explosives. I could estimate there were about three high, two and two deep. That would be about 12 boxes.

Q. And what was Mr. Nichols doing during this time?

A. He was taking some stuff out of the storage locker and putting it back into his truck. I remember specifically he was putting in a spare tire.

Q. At that storage facility, when you were shown the explosives in a box, did you have any discussion with either Mr. Nichols or Mr. McVeigh about the source of those explosives?

A. I had invited Tim and Terry to stay the night at my house 'cause I thought they were—they were sleeping in the desert. Terry declined, but Tim took me up on my offer; and that evening, Tim told me where they had gotten the explosives.

Q. What did he say?

A. He told me that him and Terry had come across this quarry that was in Kansas, near where Terry was living. They would have to drive by it like on their way to work— on Terry's way to work. He described for me the night that they went into the quarry and stole the explosives. He said it was a stormy night. I'm not sure which vehicle they were using. He told me but I forgot.

Anyway, they drove there and they took with them a Makita drill; and they tried to get into one shed, but they couldn't because of some type of antitheft device barrier that was covering the lock. So they went to another shed that did not have this device on it, and they drilled the lock and then made a few trips stealing explosives. And then it was my impression that just thereafter, they drove to Kingman with the explosives. . . .

Tim told me on the way there he was upset with Terry because Terry either almost got stopped for speeding, or he was almost in an accident, or for some reason they almost got caught by the police.

Q. With the explosives in their vehicles?

A. Yes, sir. . . .

A Target Is Chosen

Q. Approximately how long did he stay in your house?

A. For a few days. Approximately, maybe up to a week.

Q. He had previously, on a previous visit to Kingman, revealed to you the plans to blow up a building; is that right?

A. When I spoke to him by the fence, he told me that that's what they were thinking of doing, was blowing up a building.

Q. And did you have any further discussion about that plan during this visit?

A. Sometime during the month of October, before the October 31, we did have a discussion.

Q. What's the significance of October 31?

A. On that date I bought my Jeep. I bought a vehicle. And so I could place certain events either before or after that date. That's the only way I can—I can—that's as close to the dates as I can.

Q. Okay. Sometime before October 31, you had a conversation, a further conversation about the plan to blow up a building; is that correct?

A. Yes, sir.

Q. Where was that conversation?

A. In my living room.

Q. Tell us about it.

A. Tim told me that him and Terry had chosen a building in Oklahoma City, a federal building in Oklahoma City. He also told me that he had figured out how to make a truck into a bomb. He explained to me how he would arrange the barrels, 55-gallon drums in the back of that truck to form something he was calling a "shape charge."

He told me about the ratio of how to . . . fuel to ammonium nitrate to—excuse me. That that's how he would make an explosive. He told me that he would use the explosives that he had stolen from the quarry. He had drew on a piece of paper—he diagrammed the truck and the barrels, and he diagrammed how he would fuse the bomb from the front of the cab into the back area of the truck.

Q. How was he going to fuse it from the front to the back?

A. He told me he was going to just drill a hole and run a canon fuse through the hole.

Q. The hole would be where?

A. Through the back of the cab into the back portion of the truck.

Q. Did he tell you why they had selected the federal building in Oklahoma City?

A. He told me they picked that building because that was where the orders for the attack on Waco came from. He told me—he also told me that he was wanting to blow up a building to cause a general uprising in America hopefully that would knock some people off the fence into—and urge them into taking action against the federal government.

Q. Can you, using words, describe the diagram that he drew?

A. He drew a box. And then he was drawing circles to represent barrels. He drew them in the shape of a triangle. He explained to me the base of the triangle would be pointing towards the building because that is the direction the blast would travel. He was also drawing oblong circles to represent this other explosive that he was calling "sausage" that he stole from the quarry, behind the triangle to just bolster the blast.

Then he was drawing lines to represent the canon fuse.

Q. Did Mr. McVeigh tell you what time of day or night he intended to blow up this truck bomb?

A. Tim told me that he was wanting to do it at 11:00 in the morning.

Q. Did he explain why he had selected that hour?

A. He said that he wanted—I asked him why; and he said because everybody would be getting ready for lunch.

Q. Did you have any discussion about the deaths that such a bomb would cause?

A. I asked him about that right as he said that. I said, What about all the people?

And he explained to me, using the terms from the movie "Star Wars"—he explained to me that he considered all those people to be as if they were the storm troopers in the movie *Star Wars*. They may be individually innocent; but because they are part of the—the evil empire, they were—they were guilty by association.

Q. Did he tell you how he intended to acquire the materials for this bomb, other than the explosives, obviously?

A. He told me that him and Terry had already bought some ammonium nitrate. He told me the whole story about how they were using Terry's truck and they went to some type of store and that they were going to use—or they had used fake names. And Tim told me that Terry was supposed to do all the talking, but some way—you know, halfway through the buy of it, he was messing up. And Tim told me that he would have to do it from then on out.

He also explained to me how he wanted to get some fuel—he was calling anhydrous hydroxine (sic). He said he wanted to dress up like a biker and he wanted to get it at a raceway.

Q. Did you have any discussion with him as to when this bombing would occur? Not the time of day, but the date.

A. He told me that he wanted to bomb the building on the anniversary of Waco.

Q. Did he tell you why he had selected that date?

A. He didn't say specifically why.

Q. Did you know what the anniversary of Waco was?

A. I understood it to mean the anniversary of the day the fire had engulfed the compound.

Q. And did you know that date?

A. I don't remember specifically if I knew that date or not. The date has been so ingrained in my mind up till now that I don't know. It's very possible I could have.

Q. So you certainly know the date now?

A. Certainly.

Q. And the date is?

A. April 19. . . .

Making Money

Q. Did you have any further contact with Mr. McVeigh that year, 1994?

A. Yes. . . . The first call I recall is Tim calling me and asking me if I'm—was interested in making some money. He used the term "ten to the power of ten," which I understood as 10,000. I said, Sure, I was interested in that.

He said, "Okay, just, you know, wait for my further calls.". . .

Q. Did you have any further discussion about how it was you were going to make money?

A. Yes. Tim told me that alls I had to do was go to Kansas with him and he would give me—he had a bunch more [stolen] weapons just like the one he gave me and if I traveled to Kansas with him, he would give them to me [to sell at gun shows].

Q. Did you discuss how you would get to Kansas?

A. Yes, Tim told me that I should drive my Jeep to Kansas, but I didn't think that was feasible, my Jeep not being made for the highway. So I said, "Well, why don't I just ride with you and then I'll bring a duffel bag and I can put the weapons in the duffel bag and I can take a bus back, the Greyhound bus?" Tim didn't like that idea. He said, "Why don't you just rent a car?" And I was agreeable to that since I had a credit card and I was of age, so that's what we decided to do. . . .

Q. How long did it take you to drive that far?

A. Two days.

Q. So you stayed overnight someplace?

A. Yes, in Amarillo, Texas.

Q. Do—did you have any further discussion of the plans to bomb a federal building in Oklahoma City, let's say during the first day of the trip, if you recall?

A. Yes, on the first day of the trip, we were on the highway of course, passing—we were passing a truck that just happened to be a Ryder truck. Tim motioned to it and said that's the type of truck he was thinking of using, except he wanted the one size larger. He pointed to the wheel well of the truck and explained to me how the one he wanted, the back portion of the truck sat on top of the wheel instead of going around it like the one that we were looking at.

We kept passing and he also pointed to the door on the truck and said the one he was wanting to use said 18,000 pounds. The weight measurements that are on the side of the door, he pointed to them. He then told me that he was thinking that he would have to stay inside the vehicle to make sure that it was going to go off.

And I was like, "Now you're talking about committing suicide. This is stupid. What you need to do is keep standing on the street corners and telling people about this. In the next 10 years, you'd be much more effective than doing something like this."

And he told me that he didn't think talking was accomplishing anything and that he was going to sit inside the vehicle, and if anybody tried to stop it from blowing up, he was going to blow them away. . . .

Passing Through Oklahoma City

Q. Describe what you remember about the next day.

A. Well, we left Amarillo, and we were driving up to Kansas; and as we passed through Oklahoma City, Tim got off the highway saying he wanted to show me the building. We drove into downtown Oklahoma City. We drove by the back of the building first—or what I think is the back of the building and around the side—

Q. Describe this building, when you say the building.

A. I'm speaking of the federal building Tim was pointing out. What I first seen of it was the back courtyard, just a big cement courtyard with some trees; and we drove around the side of it, to the front of it. The front was just all really dark glass, like black glass.

As we drove past the front of it, Tim asked me if I thought that a truck of the size he was speaking of would fit in the— I'm not sure what it—it looks like a commercial—like a drop-off zone or just a little pull-in that's in front of the building.

And I said, "Yeah, you could probably fit three trucks in the front there."

And he drove further on, and then we turned into an alley, and he pointed out a spot where he was going to park his vehicle there. He explained to me what his plans were at that time. He said him and Terry were thinking of doing one of two things.

Excuse me, let me recant that. He said he was thinking of doing one of two things: One being Terry would follow him down in the morning, that he was planning this, and wait for him in this parking spot, or that they would drop a vehicle off there a couple days earlier and then Tim would just drive the truck down, himself, and then run to the car and get in it and drive away.

Q. Did you have any conversation with Mr. McVeigh about that parking space he'd selected?

A. Yes, I did. We were parked so that I could see down an alleyway that was more or less in the direction of the building, and I asked Tim why he wouldn't park closer—what I said was, "Why wouldn't you park down the alley?" And he said he didn't want to do that because he wanted to have a building between him and the blast. He didn't explain that any further. After that we just—we just drove away.

Putting the Blame on Terry Nichols

Lana Padilla with Ron Delpit

Shortly after Timothy McVeigh was arrested for the bombing of the federal building in Oklahoma City, police issued a warrant for Terry Nichols, an old army friend of McVeigh's, whom they believed was also involved in the bombing plot. Witnesses told the FBI that Nichols and McVeigh made and exploded small homemade bombs on a farm in Michigan owned by Nichols's brother, James. Authorities also found receipts at Nichols's home—with McVeigh's fingerprints on them—for large amounts of fertilizer and fuel, the ingredients used in the bomb that blew up the Murrah building. The FBI also suspected that Nichols, McVeigh, and perhaps another accomplice robbed a gun and coin dealer as well as nearly two dozen Midwestern banks of more than $250,000 during a two-year spree in 1994 and 1995.

Lana Padilla, Nichols's ex-wife, refuses to believe that her former husband could have been involved in the bombing. In a book cowritten with Ron Delpit, *By Blood Betrayed: My Life with Terry Nichols and Timothy McVeigh*, Padilla examines some of the evidence against Nichols. Padilla was angry that Michael Fortier, another friend of McVeigh's, was given immunity from prosecution for his testimony that he knew about the bombing plot. She believes that there are many discrepancies in the government's case against McVeigh and Nichols that cannot be explained by the evidence. She and her son, Josh, wonder why his father is in jail awaiting trial when Fortier—a man who knew about—and could have prevented—the bombing is walking around free.

Since his arrest, McVeigh had been portrayed as a stone-faced, sullen prisoner who had given nothing but his name, rank, serial number, and a statement that he was a political prisoner of war. This tactic had convinced the country that he was guilty and had something to hide. He had no family. No children. He was a loner. Background stories on McVeigh always portrayed him as angry, a demolitions man in the army and a government hater. Terry, on the other hand, had been painted as a family man. He had recently bought a house, had a wife and child and friends who spoke about him being a gentle, caring man. No one stepped forward to make similar claims about McVeigh. . . .

A Double Life?

Was there a side to Terry Nichols I didn't know?

A *New York Times* article claimed he "led a double life. On the surface he appeared to be the same old Terry Nichols—quiet, nondescript and not particularly successful. A man trying to hold his family together as he made yet another new start in Kansas." It went on to say, "But if the affidavits are to be believed, Terry Nichols was a man on a secret mission, a bomb builder who used a string of aliases as he went about methodically amassing 4,000 pounds of ammonium nitrate fertilizer, ground ammonium nitrate and diesel fuel—the ingredients of a fertilizer bomb—in rented storage lockers across Kansas."

The story finished with an underhanded dig, claiming that if "Terry Nichols did join McVeigh in constructing the bomb that destroyed the Federal Building, it may been the only plan of action he had ever carried through, from beginning to end."

Could one year in the army have transformed Terry's life that much?

I knew that a couple years after leaving the army, Terry had tried to renounce his citizenship. He sent a letter to the county clerk in Michigan, along with his voter registration card, saying "the entire political system from the local government on up through the president of the United States [was] corrupt."

That's when he declared himself a "nonresident alien non-foreigner and a stranger to the current state of the forum." It was a language familiar to right-wing extremists.

The Bank Robberies

Each day, as I went through the newspapers with my morning coffee, what most concerned me were articles intimating that Terry and McVeigh might have been connected to a string of unsolved bank robberies throughout the Midwest. A Washington bureau reporter quoted some investigators as saying the robberies "appeared to have been committed by a small group of people matching the bombing suspects' general description."

The thirteen heists had begun in Ames, Iowa, on January 25, 1994, and they all fit the same pattern. Each involved two or three white men dressed as construction workers wearing hard hats, gloves, and camouflage netting over their faces. Sometimes they wore masks. Usually they left behind something that looked like a bomb.

The robbers also displayed a certain flair for comedy, adding Santa Claus hats to their wardrobes in December when they robbed an Ohio bank.

"Yes," I exclaimed loudly, banging my hand on the table when I read about the Christmas holdup.

That was a point for Terry, and a big one.

There was no way he could have been involved in a December 1994 robbery in Ohio because he was in the Philippines at the time.

But if the bank robberies weren't the way the bombers financed their deadly mission, how did they do it? Investigators were checking every lead.

I had another thought: What if the robberies did finance their escapades? It would be possible for this to be the case and for Terry not to have been involved in the holdups.

Disturbing Thoughts

And an even more disturbing thought crept in: What if Terry knew something? What if he wasn't involved but knew who was, and was keeping quiet because he feared for his family? For Josh [his son], for Marife and Nicole [his second wife and their daughter]. After all, anyone who would blow up a building and kill 169 people would think nothing about killing two or three more.

Was he being a martyr or was I again being naive?

Terry had told some investigator that he asked McVeigh if he "was going to rob a bank." Where did he get that idea? Did he know McVeigh had robbed banks before?

An unnamed federal official said that Jennifer McVeigh had given them indications that her brother may have been involved in bank robberies. Maybe that's why she had been granted immunity in exchange for the kind of information that would be brought out at the trial.

The feds must have gotten something from her, because they had set her free, even after it had been reported that she shared her brother's antigovernment feelings, had written rebellious letters to newspapers decrying the storming of Waco, and she was aware that her brother had, years earlier, driven around in a car containing a large bomb.

She must have known he was a nutcase. . . .

Michael Fortier Enters the Picture

After a few days of something of a news blackout, the front pages were again ablaze with stories about the bombing, but two new focal points were Michael Fortier and an obscure robbery that had taken place in Arkansas on November 5, 1994, just a few days before Terry showed up at my house in Las Vegas.

FRIEND OF MCVEIGH IMPLICATES HIM IN BOMBING
FORTIER TO TESTIFY AGAINST MCVEIGH
AND NICHOLS IN PLEA BARGAIN

And the most damning of all:

MCVEIGH FRIEND IMPLICATES NICHOLS

In that story, Fortier claimed he not only knew of Tim McVeigh's plan to blow up the federal building, but was also aware that Terry Nichols would mix the chemicals that would be used in the bombing. However, he said he played no role in the April 19 disaster.

If Fortier had advance knowledge, I couldn't understand how the government could even be contemplating giving him a deal. That was insane. He could have saved the lives of 169 people.

And when he heard about it, Josh kept asking, "How can Michael be walking around free while my dad is in jail? It isn't fair." And he was right.

If, and it was a big if, Fortier knew what was going to happen, he could have prevented it. Now he was going to try to cop out. Either the government had a very weak case or they were making a big mistake in considering a negotiation.

The nation had a right to be incensed.

The *Los Angeles Times* ran a huge picture of Terry's Fort Benning infantry regiment platoon. The photo identified Terry, Michael Fortier, and Tim McVeigh. They had all been there together on June 3, 1988.

Fortier, whom Josh had identified [to the FBI as a friend of McVeigh's], was admitting that he had actually cased the federal building with Tim back in December.

A Letter to Terry

That reminded me of the December [1994] day Tim had called the house asking if Terry was back from the Philippines. I had just started writing a letter to Terry, unsure if he was dead or alive [she thought Nichols planned to commit suicide in the Philippines] and I wondered how Tim knew about the trip.

When I told him about Terry's whereabouts, he said, "That's too bad," sounding a bit hyper. "I really need to talk to him. Do you have a number for him in the Philippines?"

"No, but I have an address," I replied.

"I'll write to him, but I guess I'd better do it in code, because there are a lot of nosy people." I gave him the only address I had for Terry. . . .

When I hung up with Tim, I continued with the letter,

hoping and praying that Terry would be alive to receive it. I felt chills run up my arms.

Not until months later did the pieces seem to fall into place. Tim had cased the building with Fortier and could possibly have been looking for someone to drive the get-away car or help with the bomb.

This probably explains why he then called another King-man pal, one James Rosencrans, who has since told authorities that on the same day McVeigh called me, he called and asked Rosencrans if he wanted to help him by driving a car or truck in a deal he was working on in the Midwest.

I mentioned McVeigh's call in the letter I was writing to Terry, telling him that Tim sounded desperate. I also told him there were a lot of people who loved him and that Josh needed him, and included a Christmas card and a program from Josh's Christmas play. Perhaps, if what he was feeling was just depression, a positive letter might help bring him to his senses.

As I continued reading the paper, I learned that investi-gators reported that Fortier resembled one of several men who had "cased" a federal building in Omaha several weeks before the Oklahoma City explosion. Witnesses said the men asked specific questions about the Federal Bureau of Alcohol, Tobacco and Firearms offices in the building, in-cluding queries about the number of agents and how many were armed.

Another Robbery

The other new focal point in the news, the robbery in Arkansas, did not capture my attention immediately, but as I read details of it I began to see how authorities could think it definitely had some connection to McVeigh and maybe to Terry as well.

The victim, Roger Moore, a gun and coin dealer, had stepped out his back door only to be confronted by a man in camouflage gear and a black ski mask. According to the po-lice report, there were probably two assailants. Moore was bound with duct tape and blindfolded while the robbers ransacked his home, stealing cash and goods worth more than $60,000, including seventy guns, silver and gold bars, some precious stones, and an undisclosed number of gold coins.

Although the fifty-nine-year-old Moore could not identify either of the thieves, he did tell police Tim McVeigh had visited him on several occasions and was familiar with his gun collection.

There was the link to McVeigh, aka Tim Tuttle, aka Joe Kyle and who knows what else.

There were never any claims that Terry knew Moore, and Moore failed to identify Terry in a lineup, but the FBI claimed to have found a very damaging tie-in. While searching Terry's house in Herington, agents claimed to have found a safety-deposit-box key belonging to Moore that was stolen in the robbery.

Lawyers will probably be able to explain the key away, but I couldn't. Then again, maybe Tim left it there. He had visited Terry in Herington. The evidence was powerful, but it was still circumstantial. The FBI also noted that in the months following the robbery McVeigh had "wads" of cash and paid cash for everything he did.

A Lot of Discrepancies

I couldn't come up with an explanation for a lot of discrepancies. Why did Terry need aliases, such as Ted Parker and Mike Havens? It wasn't illegal to use an alias, but normal people didn't have any reason to.

When Tim was stopped and arrested the morning of the bombing, he was driving the same yellow Mercury that had supposedly broken down and necessitated his call to Terry asking for a ride. Why would he make a friend drive 480 miles roundtrip from Herington to Oklahoma City if his car could be fixed that easily?

Assuming it was ever really broken in the first place.

And the television set he had brought from Las Vegas. How important was it, really? Sure, Josh watched movies on it the next day, but Terry's house had no antenna and no cable hookup. Odd, but nothing necessarily suspicious. Cable can be ordered, and Terry ordered it on Thursday, the day after the bombing, and an antenna can be erected with little trouble. And as Josh told the FBI, Marife had been nagging his dad about getting a TV.

Another reason some people have a tough time believing the case against Terry is the fact that he spent the morning of April 19 around Herington, picking up business cards, registering his truck with the state, and calling on a couple of local shops, asking about their interest in buying government surplus.

Those are not the actions of a guilty man.

Waiting for an Explanation

Yet Terry Lynn Nichols sits in an abandoned wing at El Reno Federal Prison. The public now knows more about his personal life, his small accomplishments, and ultimate failings than a man so private would ever have revealed, yet still he makes no statements. Not even to his loved ones.

Michael Fortier has now made his deal. He'll testify against Terry and McVeigh in exchange for a more lenient sentence and immunity for his wife.

Meanwhile Terry sits and waits, the surveillance cameras recording his every move. The world is still waiting for an explanation, and Josh's question now begs for an answer more than ever: "Why is Michael Fortier out and my dad still in jail?"

The Evidence Does Not Make Sense

Robert Nigh

After all the evidence had been presented to the jury in the McVeigh trial, the prosecuting and defense attorneys gave their closing arguments, in which they reviewed the evidence that had been presented. Because the prosecution bore the burden of proving that Timothy McVeigh committed the crime, the prosecution presented its closing statement first, followed by the defense's closing argument.

Robert Nigh was one of the attorneys defending McVeigh and he presented a portion of the defense's closing statement. He tried to show that the prosecution did not meet its burden of proving that McVeigh committed the bombing. Nigh attacked the methods the FBI used to examine the evidence; he argued that the agency had determined what it wanted the evidence to show before it was even examined. In addition, no safeguards were taken to prevent contamination of the evidence. Therefore, Nigh concludes, the entire forensics evidence is suspect and so the state did not meet its burden of proof.

M r. Nigh: Thank you, your Honor.
May it please the Court, ladies and gentlemen. . . .
Somehow, some way, magically, at the time of this explosion, an explosion that you know from the evidence, that you heard from [FBI Special Agent] Steven Burmeister and Linda Jones, the [explosives] experts called by the Government to testify in this case, that at the time of an explosion,

Robert Nigh, closing statement, *USA v. Timothy James McVeigh*, Criminal Action No. 96-CR-68, May 29, 1997.

if the blast wave is 5,000 feet per second, so we can use a number, it moves away 90 degrees in every direction at the same speed from the center of the explosion—somehow, some way, magically, these crystals that evaporate at about 200 degrees—ammonium nitrate—excuse me—vaporizes at about 200 degrees—made it through the heat, waited until somehow Q507 [a piece of the Ryder truck side panel used as evidence in the trial] was sheared into about 10 percent of its original piece, moving away at 5,000 feet per second; these crystals, these magical crystals, waited until it was sheared away, picked up speed faster than the blast wave, caught Q507, and embedded themselves on the interior side of a piece of wood moving away at 5,000 feet per second. Magic. Magic.

Smoke and Mirrors

More like smoke and mirrors, ladies and gentlemen. Q507 then on its magical journey travels 184 feet into the parking lot, where the Government claims they found it. In between the time that the Government found it, or the citizen found it, and Q507 was analyzed, a torrential downpour occurred in Oklahoma City on April 19, a downpour so heavy, so strong, that Special Agent Burmeister's plane had to land in Little Rock, it couldn't land in Oklahoma City; a torrential downpour so heavy and strong that the evidence in this case—that the evidence has shown that the wind was blowing 30 to 40 miles per hour, but not around Q507. It just laid there in the parking lot, didn't get blown, and obviously didn't get wet because crystals of ammonium nitrate—the hydroscopic crystals of ammonium nitrate that soak up water and melt in water and evaporate away made it. They lasted through the storm, and they made it through the blast. Magic.

Ladies and gentlemen, it is more logical that the crystals that were found on Q507 made their way onto Q507 after the blast. I don't know where they came from. They may have come from the ammonium-nitrate-based firefighting tools that were used by the firefighters in Oklahoma City. As Steven Burmeister testified, ammonium nitrate and nitrate ions can naturally bond together and form a crystal. That may have happened. I do not know.

But it is not my burden, it is not Timothy McVeigh's burden, to prove anything. The Government has the burden of proof in this case and in every case, and they always will. They have not proven to you the origin of the crystals on Q507, although they have tried. Although they have made a valiant effort to prove to you that these crystals were a result of ammonium nitrate prills [small pellets formed after molten spray hardens] they have not done that.

And let's talk about the final failing with the prills of— the crystals of ammonium nitrate that Steven Burmeister found on Q507. He gets it to the lab. Here they are. The testimony in this courtroom was they were embedded. You know now after Dr. John Lloyd [an English forensic scientist] had to endure that cross-examination alleging that he was making up that Steven Burmeister said it was a glaze— you know now by the evidence in this case that that's what he wrote in 1995: Not embedded, glazed. What you know now is Steven Burmeister did in fact—and I believe it that he did pull a crystal off of Q507 and drop it in the magic juice and it turned purple or blue or whatever color it turns.

Now, we've got a receipt that shows that the purchase of ammonium nitrate in Kansas was ICI [a manufacturer of explosives in] Joplin prills manufactured in 1994. So what are we going to do? Steven Burmeister is going to prove to you that these crystals originated as ICI Joplin prills; so he takes Q507 to ICI to be analyzed. The magic crystals, the crystals that so magically appeared, have so magically disappeared. They're gone. ICI doesn't get to test them. Dr. John Lloyd doesn't get to test them. Linda Jones doesn't get to test them. There is only one person on the face of the earth that got an opportunity to test the crystals of ammonium nitrate on Q507: Special Agent Steven Burmeister.

Not Sound Forensic Science

It doesn't matter, though. What did he tell you about the loss of the ammonium and nitrate crystals? What did he tell you about losing somehow the most important piece of forensic evidence in this case, the only piece of forensic evidence that they could bring you from Oklahoma City? What did he tell you about losing it? It didn't matter; I was through testing it.

Is that sound forensic science? Is that the type of science that you would expect from an objective forensic scientist? It's more like the type of science that you would expect from a special agent of the Federal Bureau of Investigation who had long before the testing made up his mind about the facts of this case.

He took no effort to preserve those crystals, but he did test them. And when he tested them, he found substances consistent with the coating of ammonium nitrate prills, aluminum and sulfur.

So we've got that evidence. Let's go to ICI. Let's test the prills from Joplin in 1994 and let's find out what the coating is on them.

What did he tell you? Talc. And what you found from the evidence, what you know from that witness stand from Steven Burmeister, is that a component part of talc is magnesium. Do you recall the testimony as the last witness in the case, the last piece of evidence that you heard from the witness stand, Steven Burmeister telling you about the crystals and the testing on Q507 that he found no magnesium? Ladies and gentlemen, if the aluminum and the sulfur are the coating of the prill, he would have found magnesium, also.

I do not know where the crystals on Q507 originated from. I do not know how the crystals on Q507 got glazed over the surface of Q507, but we do know from the evidence in this case that those crystals did not originate from ammonium nitrate prills manufactured by ICI Joplin in 1994.

Testing for PETN

Now, the lab went on to test some additional evidence: the clothes, Mr. McVeigh's two T-shirts, and his pants. They took an interesting route to the lab. They were seized in Noble County. They were not evidence. They were clothes. They were Mr. McVeigh's clothes, a man arrested for carrying a weapon; so they were thrown in a paper bag and left alone in the room upstairs where the attorneys meet with the clients and where the trustees sometime hang out.

I do not allege and I do not stand before you and state that anybody in Noble County intentionally contaminated those clothes with PETN [a high explosive used in ammunition, land mines, and detonation (det) cord]. I only tell you that somehow, PETN got on the clothes. You may have noticed by now, you may have wondered throughout the course of this trial, what home does PETN have in this case? It's been found in three places: Mr. McVeigh's inside T-shirt, Mr. McVeigh's outside T-shirt, and the pockets of Mr. McVeigh's blue jeans.

The Government didn't bring you any PETN from Oklahoma City. The Government didn't bring you any PETN

Lashing Out Against Government Abuse of Civil Liberties

After the jury found Timothy McVeigh guilty on all eleven counts, a sentencing hearing was held. Both the prosecution and the defense presented witnesses and argued why or why not the jury should select the death penalty as McVeigh's punishment.

After the testimony and legal arguments, but before the jury's sentence was revealed, McVeigh was given an opportunity to give a statement to the court. Many people hoped or expected that McVeigh would apologize for his crime or offer condolences to the survivors. But McVeigh chose as his statement a portion of a dissenting opinion from 1928 by Supreme Court Justice Louis D. Brandeis. Brandeis was a strong supporter of the right to privacy, and he strenuously objected to a ruling in a case known as Olmstead v. United States *in which the court upheld the use of wiretaps to convict bootleggers. McVeigh quoted just a very short fragment of the opinion, hoping, perhaps, that people would look up the rest, in which Brandeis wrote: "If the government becomes a law breaker, it breeds contempt for the law; it in-*

from any of the storage units that were searched by the FBI lab. The Government didn't bring you any PETN from Mr. McVeigh's car. Now, Steven Burmeister took that witness stand and he told you that he had enough PETN on his hands—and he's right-handed. That's important: We've got more in the right pocket. But we've got to ask a question about that—and I digress for a moment if I may. This lab does no quantitative analysis. You heard that more than once in this case. How does Steven Burmeister know there is more PETN in the right pocket than the left? How does Steven Burmeister know how much PETN was on any item he checked in this case? He didn't try to find out. He doesn't want to find out.

But that's okay. We've got more PETN in the right pocket, because he's right-handed. He saw him writing here

---

vites every man to become a law unto himself; it invites anarchy. . . . To declare that the government may commit crimes in order to secure the conviction of a private criminal—would bring terrible retribution."

THE COURT: There is provision for the Court to hear statements from counsel for the defendant, from the defendant, and also counsel for the Government. And I intend to follow that rule. . . .

Mr. McVeigh, you have the right to make any statement you wish to make. Do you wish to make a statement?

THE DEFENDANT: Yes, your Honor, briefly.

THE COURT: Would you please come to the lectern to make that statement.

You may speak, Mr. McVeigh.

THE DEFENDANT: If the Court please, I wish to use the words of Justice Brandeis dissenting in *Olmstead* to speak for me. He wrote, "Our Government is the potent, the omnipresent teacher. For good or for ill, it teaches the whole people by its example." That's all I have.

Timothy McVeigh, sentencing hearing, *USA v. Timothy James McVeigh*, Criminal Action No. 96-CR-68, August 13, 1997.

at the counsel table and used that against him and said that's consistent with him having more PETN in the right pocket. If that's the case, if he had more PETN on his right hand than his left, where is the PETN from Mr. McVeigh's steering wheel? The sticky substance . . . that would have transferred when he grabbed his steering wheel to drive a car: Where is it? There is not any.

Where is the PETN that would have been on the gear shift knob when he shifted the car into drive or reverse or neutral or low? There isn't any.

Where is the PETN that would have been on the door handle when he opened the door? There isn't any. And finally, and most importantly, because they can say all day that it doesn't matter that it wasn't on his car, it certainly should have been on his fingerprint card when the Noble County Jail took his fingerprints. There was no PETN, no ammonium nitrate, no residue of any kind on Mr. McVeigh's fingerprint card taken before he had an opportunity to take a shower at the Noble County Jail.

My friends, if Tim McVeigh had cut det cord and got it all over his shirts and on his hands, it would have been somewhere else other than his clothes.

Do you recall Dr. John Lloyd testifying about the testing done by this lab, by the FBI lab, the Federal Bureau of Investigation, on the fingernail scrapings taken from Tim McVeigh at the Noble County Jail? No PETN. They took a hair sample from Tim McVeigh at the Noble County Jail tested by Steven Burmeister and the crack scientists at the FBI lab. No PETN.

PETN does not seem to have a home in this case, but it does; and we know now where it does. . . . The last witness in this case, Steven Burmeister, testified and he told you that he knew—he already knew that the bullets that Tim McVeigh was carrying in his pockets and in the clip on his gun were manufactured with PETN. That's why Tim McVeigh had PETN in his pockets. That's why Tim McVeigh had PETN on his T-shirts. If you will recall, Charlie Hanger [the police officer who arrested McVeigh for driving without a license plate on his car] found Tim McVeigh wearing a handgun with a shoulder holster that would have rubbed on the shirts. When you fire a weapon, it leaves a residue. That residue in this case was nitroglycerin and PETN.

Steven Burmeister told you that nitroglycerin is—evaporates very rapidly. It's not inconsistent that that shirt only had the sticky substance PETN left on it.

And finally, with respect to the PETN, where is the testing on Mr. McVeigh's knife? How many times in this case have we heard—and today in Mr. Mackey's closing argument did you hear that you have to cut the det cord with a knife? When you cut the det cord, the PETN spills out and gets all over you.

Where is the forensic testing on Mr. McVeigh's knife? If Mr. McVeigh had cut det cord containing PETN enough to spill out on his clothes, his shirt, drop into his pants pockets, it would have been on his knife.

If PETN was on Mr. McVeigh's knife, Mr. Burmeister would have told you about it.

There is no PETN on the shoes.

Ammonium Nitrate

How about ammonium nitrate, ladies and gentlemen? Now, we've discussed the magic of Q507 and the crystals glazed upon it. Where is the rest of it?

The Government's theory in this case is that Timothy McVeigh participated in pouring 4,000 pounds of ammonium nitrate into barrels, barrels with holes in them about that big. Where is the ammonium nitrate on Tim McVeigh? There is no ammonium nitrate in his fingernail scrapings. There is no ammonium nitrate in his hair sample. There is no ammonium nitrate on either shirt. There is no ammonium nitrate on his pants. There is no ammonium nitrate on his shoes. There is no ammonium nitrate in his car. There is no ammonium nitrate in any of the storage sheds.

That's okay. He showered at the Noble County Jail, if you will recall the testimony; so if I understand the theory that the Government is asking you to buy into in this case, it is that Tim McVeigh poured 4,000 pounds of ammonium nitrate into barrels with holes about that big, covered with . . . ammonium nitrate. Do you recall the testimony of [mining engineer] Mr. [Paul] Rydlund that it's dusty; that you can't breathe it or you might get sick? Do you recall the testimony of Mr. Rydlund that too much exposure to ammonium nitrate will cause a skin rash? Do you recall that Tim McVeigh had no rash when he was arrested? Do you recall the bag, the empty bag of ammonium nitrate that the Government introduced about the third day of trial in this case? They offered it to show you what the bag looked like and that it says "Explosives" on it. I offer it, ladies and gentlemen, for the ammonium nitrate stuck on the bottom of the bag of the Government's exhibit.

I offer it, ladies and gentlemen, to show you that these prills get everywhere. I offer it, ladies and gentlemen, to show you that Timothy McVeigh, had he poured 4,000 pounds of ammonium nitrate into barrels, would be covered in ammonium nitrate. I offer it, ladies and gentlemen, so that when you analyze the size of the prill on the bottom of the bag, you will know that surely one or more of them should have gotten lodged in his boots.

But that's okay. Timothy McVeigh showered at the Noble County Jail. It doesn't matter that we found no ammonium nitrate, because he showered. It is the theory of this case that he poured the 4,000 pounds of ammonium nitrate into the barrels, said, My gosh, I'm covered in ammonium nitrate, I'm going to go home, shower, change clothes, come back, cut the det cord, get PETN all over me, not change, and go deliver the bomb.

Contamination

Ladies and gentlemen, we must use our common sense when we analyze evidence. We must use our common sense when we analyze the testimony of the experts called by the Government in a case this serious. And this is not logical.

The FBI lab, as I said earlier, is a ship without a rudder. It's adrift without a sail and a captain. The clothes in this case were brought in in a cardboard box checked in by Mr. [Brett] Mills [a physical science technician for the FBI]; and he took them and put them on the floor, a floor that you know now has never been tested for contamination. It doesn't matter. We're not contaminated. We know we're not contaminated because we say so.

That's not enough. That doesn't cut it. This is a criminal prosecution. The FBI lab has a higher burden than just to say, We're not contaminated; than just to say, regardless of the fact that Dr. Fred Whitehurst, after eleven years of faithful service [as a supervisory special agent for the FBI] has found contamination in this lab, We're not contaminated.

Compare and contrast this lab with Linda Jones', the other Government expert, the Government expert called in in place of Dave Williams to testify in this case. What does her lab do? How does her lab protect from contamination? The first thing that lab did, the DERA [Defense Evaluation and Research Agency] in London—the first thing they did was say, We know that any trace analysis facility in explosives residue is going to get contaminated. We understand that. We appreciate that, and now let's work within it. Now let's do something about it, understanding that there is a problem, a problem that we will never be able to do away with. So what did they do? They said 10 nanograms, which as I recall—and I'm sorry my chemistry class was not that good—I can't recall how small; but as I recall, it's about a spec of dust. 10 nanograms of contamination is all we will stand, and we will test this lab every week. And if we get more than 10 nanograms, we will stop in that area and we will clean.

If we get test results within 10 nanograms—in other words, when I run my questioned sample through my GC/Chem and my IMS and my FTIR and all the other acronyms that I've forgotten, if I get less than 10 nanograms on my quantitative analysis, I'm going to report it. I'm going to tell the prosecutor in that case that the results I got could be a part of random contamination.

We don't do that at the FBI. We don't want to do that at the FBI, because Special Agent Burmeister is just that: He is a special agent. A professional forensic scientist would take the effort, the time, and the energy to do the quantitative analysis necessary so that juries like yourself will know for sure if the information and the evidence that you're getting is clean and clear of contamination.

But we don't want to know that. We don't want to take the time and the effort and the energy to do the quantitative analysis because it's too hard. It takes too much time. We're busy.

Are you going to rely on that? You can't. You can't. The lab has an obligation to you as jurors to give you professional and objective information. They did not do that. Linda Jones' lab restricts the visitors who can enter the trace analysis area. Not our lab. Let's take the military in from all over the world.

Linda Jones' lab makes you wash your hands before you can come into the locked door. Not our lab. Come on in, boys. We don't care if you just came from the bomb range. We're not going to test you. Doesn't matter anyway. We're not contaminated.

Linda Jones' lab makes you put on gloves and Tyvex suits and cover your shoes. Not our lab. Come on in, boys. Check it out. Touch whatever you want, walk across the carpet we've never shampooed.

Ladies and gentlemen, that's not a professional forensic lab. Linda Jones' lab is. I applaud the efforts that she's taken and her lab has taken to ensure the integrity of the results.

It is unfortunate that in this country the Federal Bureau of Investigation, the group that claims to have the finest forensic lab in the world, is so shabbily maintained and so shabbily managed.

We brought Dr. Lloyd in from London, someone who knows how a lab should operate, someone who knows how a lab should work, to review the 5,000 pages of notes produced by the Government in this case. What did he tell you? He told you that with respect to the shirts and the . . . pants, he might have tested them just to see; but the route they took, the way they were maintained, the way they were handled by Roger Martz and Brett Mills taken through the lab without proper forensic trace analysis testing, he would not even have reported the results. That's professionalism. That is a forensic scientist who understands his obligation and his duty is to produce reliable and objective forensic results.

What did Linda Jones tell you about Q507? She certainly would have liked to have known that . . . Roger Martz had tested Q507. She certainly would have liked to have known the results of the testing by Roger Martz. Wouldn't you like to know the testing by Roger Martz, the results of the forensic testing performed in this case by the former chief of the Chemistry/Toxicology Unit? Wouldn't you like to know that? It is a shame that the Government did not call the former chief of the Chemistry/Toxicology Unit to testify in this case. Sure, I could have called him. But why? I don't have a burden. It's their burden to prove that the testing they did in this case is fair, is reliable, and is objective. It seems reasonable to conclude that they felt they could prove that easier without the former chief of the Chemistry/Toxicology Unit, Roger Martz. . . .

Evidence to Fit a Theory

Ladies and gentlemen, the actions of the FBI lab in this case constitute the rush to judgment that Mr. [Jones] was talking to you about a moment ago. They made up their minds on April 19 that this was an ammonium nitrate and fuel oil bomb, yet they have no fuel oil to show you, they have no nitromethane to show you, and they have no forensic evidence to show you that it was. But they decided that before they did the testing; and you know that they did, because if you will recall the memorandum that Dr. Whitehurst wrote to Steven Burmeister on May 8, 1995, when he told him he could look for ammonium nitrate prills in the building, that was before he had tested Q507. They decided early on what they were going to do, and they made the evidence fit their theory.

The lab is adrift without a rudder and without a sail. Can you imagine going to the doctor feeling that you have a heart problem and he does a blood test and says, You've got some cholesterol, but I didn't find out how much. I'm not really sure if my machine was clean. Let's go ahead and open you up and do a bypass. Would you hesitate for just a moment before you let the doctor cut you open with that advice? I suggest that you would.

Not Vengeance, but Justice

George W. Bush

George W. Bush is the forty-third president of the United States. The following selection is his statement following the execution of Timothy McVeigh. Bush asserts that although McVeigh has died, the pain lives on for his victims and their families. However, Americans can now rest in the knowledge, he asserts, that justice has been done.

This morning the United States of America carried out the severest sentence for the gravest of crimes. The victims of the Oklahoma City bombing have been given not vengeance but justice. And one young man met the fate he chose for himself 6 years ago.

For the survivors of the crime and for the families of the dead, the pain goes on. Final punishment of the guilty cannot alone bring peace to the innocent. It cannot recover the loss or balance the scales, and it is not meant to do so. Today every living person who was hurt by the evil done in Oklahoma City can rest in the knowledge that there has been a reckoning.

At every point, from the morning of April 19, 1995, to this hour, we have seen the good that overcomes evil. We saw it in the rescuers who saved and suffered with the victims. We have seen it in a community that has grieved and held close the memory of the lost. We have seen it in the work of detectives, marshals, and police, and we've seen it

George W. Bush, remarks on the execution of Timothy McVeigh, June 11, 2001.

in the courts. Due process ruled: The case was proved; the verdict was calmly reached; and the rights of the accused were protected and observed to the full and to the end. Under the laws of our country, the matter is concluded.

Life and history bring tragedies, and often they cannot be explained. But they can be redeemed. They are redeemed by dispensing justice, though eternal justice is not ours to deliver. By remembering those who grieve, including Timothy McVeigh's mother, father, and sisters, and by trusting in purposes greater than our own, may God in his mercy grant peace to all—to the lives that were taken 6 years ago, to the lives that go on, and to the life that ended today.

Chapter 6

The Memorial

Chapter Preface

M emorials are symbols that a nation has not forgotten—
and will not forget—an event. They can be permanent
symbols, such as statues, tombs, pyramids, walls, or arches;
or intangible ones, such as lists of names or a collection of
photos on the Internet. Spontaneous memorial sites are familiar around the world, from the crosses that are often
erected at scenes of fatal accidents to the massive collection
of flower bouquets left at the American embassy in London
following the terrorist attacks on September 11, 2001. The
memorial in Oklahoma City started out as an impromptu
site, with stuffed toys, flowers, and personal messages for
the victims—or to no one in particular—left at the chain-
link fence that surrounded the destroyed building. The spontaneous outpouring of grief allows people to show that those
who lost their lives were valued and loved and missed.

After the building was destroyed, a 350-member task
force composed of survivors, victims, and their family members; civic leaders; and architects met to begin the process
of establishing a permanent memorial to the victims of the
bombing. The Oklahoma City Memorial Foundation's mission statement was the cornerstone in choosing an appropriate memorial for the site. "We come here to remember
those who were killed, those who survived and those
changed forever. May all who leave here know the impact
of violence. May this memorial offer comfort, strength,
peace, hope and serenity." The memorial design chosen has
many different components—all meant to honor and remember those who were affected in some way by the bombing at 9:02 A.M. at the Alfred P. Murrah Federal Building on
April 19, 1995. The mementos left behind by visitors are
gathered up, archived, stored, and occasionally displayed inside the educational museum on the site.

A Memorial to Honor the Heroes and Victims

Bill Clinton

> Following the selection of a memorial design for the bombing of the federal building in Oklahoma City, Oklahoma Representative Frank Lucas authored a bill to designate the bomb site a national memorial and a part of the National Park Service. Bill Clinton, the forty-second president of the United States, at a ceremony in which he accepted a sapling from the elm tree at the bombing site, spoke of how the bombing made Americans realize what was important in life and how they came together to help those in need. He also commended the memorial design and urged the passage of the bill making the site a national memorial.

Thank you, [Oklahoma City] Mayor [Ronald J. Norick] . . . for your extraordinary leadership in a very difficult time.

Thank you Robert Johnson [chairman of the Oklahoma City Memorial Foundation] for taking on this [memorial] project and seeing it through with such care and ability and love. . . .

I'd like to thank . . . all the people who worked so hard on this from the federal government in the days and months and for a long time afterward. And . . . thank you for the sapling [from the Survivors' Tree].

Bill Clinton, remarks at the Oklahoma City Bombing Memorial Ceremony, August 13, 1997.

A Great Gift to America

I will take good care of it. I have already been advised by the people who run the grounds here that I cannot run out and plant it in the hot Washington summer but that we can keep it in our greenhouse and then in October, we will plant it alongside the dogwood [planted in memory of the bombing victims] on the White House lawn.

It is a great gift to the American people. It comes from what is a true tree of life, and that tree will always remind us of the city, the people, who've bent, but did not break.

We Will Never Forget

And Hillary and I will never forget what happened on April 19th, 1995, or our trips there afterward, the losses people endured, the heroism of the rescue workers, the compassion of the neighbors and the friends from around America.

And I think we now know that, in spite of everything, we did not lose America. And America, I think, is very proud of the people of Oklahoma City and the entire state of Oklahoma. I think there's not a citizen in our country that didn't identify with the people in that awful moment and in the days afterward.

Every one of us who ever came there and saw you wearing the pictures of your loved ones, we saw our children and our parents, and our sisters and our brothers. And we owe you an enormous debt because you have given us a gift, too, of reminding us what is truly important.

I've talked to Governor [Frank] Keating about this on times. You know, we went to college together, and we sort of weren't in the same political party back then either. And the issues that we deal with now make the ones dealt with then seem small. But the truth is, here in this town, where we do a lot of things that are very important, we argue and we debate and we ferociously struggle over things that, in that awful moment, were stripped of all their pretense and significance.

And we were reminded once again, as we are today, about the things which really count in life, the things which God has given to all of us, the things which no one can take away, and the things that, perhaps, we'll do a better job of never forgetting in the pressure of our daily lives when we sometimes are fooled into thinking that what we're doing now will be of some lasting benefit more profound than the simple gift of life and the human spirit that we've been given, and that it is our charge to preserve as best we can for all of our fellow citizens.

And that was a gift that the people of Oklahoma City gave to me, that your dignity and generosity, and yours, Mayor, and all the people gave to me. And I'm very grateful to you for it. And I think that maybe it makes all of us who were so moved by it a little more effective and a little more human, day in and day out, than we otherwise might have been.

And for those of you who endured terrible losses, perhaps at least you can know that your loved ones—and what they gave up—live on in all of us trying just a little harder every day to be better people and to do the right thing than we might have otherwise done.

I want to also say that I have been terrifically impressed by the design for this memorial. It is elegant. It is symbolic. It manages to focus on this act of unconscionable violence and still honor the valor of the people of the community and the lives of the victims in a setting of reflection and peace that should leave people when they go through it feeling stronger rather than weaker. And that is no small task.

So I'm glad [that memorial architects] Hans and Torrey [Butzer] you're here, and I wish Mr. [Sven] Berg was here. This is an inspired effort. And you, too, will give over time millions of people a gift that is truly priceless.

A Process of Healing

Let me say, too—Mr. Johnson talked about this—but I want to compliment the process. I have no doubt that the totally open and democratic nature of this process, reaching out to the family members and the survivors every step of the way, was absolutely indispensable to the healing of the people who were affected by what happened. I also have no doubt that it gave you a better memorial, a more powerful, a more profound, more lasting memory.

I also understand that there are several people here who have made substantial financial contributions to make it possible for the groundbreaking to occur next April [1998].

And I want to thank all of them. And having been involved in matters like this in the past, I want to encourage others to help them until the full cost is met.

Let me say that there's something we should do at the national level, as well. We all know that the Oklahoma City bombing was an attack not just on the people, a city, a state, but the nation and—as the mayor said—on what we stand for, how we govern ourselves, the values we live by.

The Congress is now considering legislation to make all three components of the Oklahoma City memorial a national monument and part of our national park system. I strongly support that goal. The tragedy was a national one, and the memorial should be recognized and embraced and supported by the nation.

Thanks to the Oklahoma City Memorial Foundation and the family members and the survivors, we have now reached another crucial stage in our recovery.

And we have now a memorial that I hope will be part of our National Park Service, a memorial of true power and amazing grace.

I'm grateful to all of you. I look forward to the success of the legislation. And again, I say you have helped our nation, and for that, we are very grateful.

Oklahoma City Needs a Memorial

Ronald J. Norick

The bomb that exploded outside the Alfred P. Murrah Federal Building in Oklahoma City on April 19, 1995, destroyed more than the federal building. More than three hundred buildings were damaged in the blast and twelve buildings had to be completely demolished. The bombing devastated Oklahoma City's downtown. Many businesses were reluctant to rebuild and the area remains a wasteland.

Ronald J. Norick, the mayor of Oklahoma City, urged Congress to pass legislation designating the bomb site as a national memorial and incorporating the memorial into the National Park Service. In the following address, he argues that making the bomb site a national memorial would send a message to the residents and businesses of Oklahoma City—and to Americans in general—that the healing process has begun. Businesses would be more eager to rebuild if they knew that the former federal building will become a national memorial.

Mr. Chairman and Members of the Subcommittee. I am Ronald J. Norick, Mayor of Oklahoma City, Oklahoma. On behalf of the members of the City Council, I would like to thank you for this opportunity to testify before you today.

As you know, the bombing of the Alfred P. Murrah Federal Building in downtown Oklahoma City on April 19, 1995, devastated the lives of Oklahoma City residents in a

Ronald J. Norick, testimony before the Subcommittee on National Parks and Public Lands of the Committee on Resources, U.S. House of Representatives, September 9, 1997.

way unlike any other event in the history of the United States. I will focus my testimony on the impact the bombing had on Oklahoma City and why the proposed legislation is so important to our city.

An Attack on All Americans

This legislation will not only benefit Oklahoma City, it will benefit all Americans. While this event occurred in Oklahoma City, it was an attack on all Americans. It was an attack on all people who believe in the principles of this nation. People from every state in the nation as well as thousands of people from outside the United States have visited the memorial site. Hundreds of people can be found at the site every day, in all kinds of weather, at all times of the day and night.

This event touched people not just in the United States, but around the world. Thousands of items were sent to my office from people from around the world. It has been over 2 years since the bombing, visitation and inquiries about the site have not declined. Thousands of people visit the site weekly. More than a million people have visited the site since the bombing leaving a piece of them at the chain link fence that surrounds the building footprint. They have left hundreds of thousands of items including messages, toys, flowers and shirts off their back as they try to express their sympathy, their compassion and somehow understand that this could have happened anywhere in the United States.

For reference, the site is not more than a mile from the intersection of two of the country's major interstate highways, together carrying over 200,000 vehicles daily. Visitation will not decrease. The construction of the memorial and learning center will result in an increase in visitation, adding impetus to the City's efforts to improve the appearance and vitality of downtown Oklahoma City.

This legislation granting National Park status will recognize the sacred nature of the site and its significance to all Americans. This site of a tragic event has become a special place in our nation's identity. It cannot, will not and should not be forgotten. This is why the City strongly supports this legislation.

Other than the loss of life, and the accompanying impact on the lives of those touched by those losses, the bombing of the Alfred P. Murrah Federal Building tore the heart out of our city. More than 300 structures were damaged and 12 buildings had to be demolished in the heart of our downtown. Rebuilding has been difficult as property owners and tenants, forced out of the area by damages to their properties, have been reluctant to reestablish in downtown Oklahoma City. Many have not had the finances. Special funding provided by Congress in 1995 has been absolutely vital to our rebuilding process. The recovery has been slow, and there still remains a very visible hole in the City's fabric.

The Memorial Will Provide Healing

The Oklahoma City Memorial, in conjunction with the passage of this legislation, will do much to heal that hole. It sends a powerful message to the people of Oklahoma City and to the Nation that the healing process is well underway, and that investment in the renewal of downtown makes good economic and civic sense.

Knowing that within a year, building will begin on a world class Memorial on the site of the Murrah Building and that it will be designated a National Park, permits the City to be more specific in targeting development in the downtown area, especially in the severely impacted district surrounding the Memorial.

The redevelopment of several of the larger buildings most heavily damaged by the bombing will now be possible. The City can also begin planning for traffic control, parking, streetscaping, sidewalk improvements, directional signage and other public improvements required to cater to the restructured business district and visitors to the site. Much of this planning has been on hold as the City and property owners have struggled with the task of making this area whole again. That hold will be lifted by this legislation. Private investors who have been holding back until they know the future of the area, can also begin their reconstruction plans.

The City strongly supports this legislation's establishment of the Oklahoma City National Memorial Trust. It is vital to those most directly affected by the events of April 19, 1995, that the story of this tragic event be managed locally. The Trust is the best vehicle for doing so.

Let me say again, the tragedy that befell Oklahoma City on April 19, 1995, was not just a tragedy for those of us in Oklahoma. It was a tragedy that affected the whole nation. The effect of that tragedy is felt no less today, over 2 years later. It is only fitting that a tragedy of such national significance be recognized as such, and the legislation I speak in support of today provides that recognition. The city of Oklahoma City strongly supports this legislation, and we will be happy to do whatever is necessary to support its passage.

The Meaning of the Memorial

Hans Butzer

> The Oklahoma City Memorial Foundation was established to choose an appropriate memorial for the federal building in Oklahoma City. A design competition resulted in 624 entries from all fifty states and twenty-three countries that were winnowed down to five finalists. A committee of fifteen people—which included survivors—chose the winning design submitted by a Berlin-based architecture firm. Hans Butzer, his wife Torrey Butzer (a native of Oklahoma), and their colleague, Sven Berg, were the principal designers.
>
> Hans Butzer explained his design at a congressional hearing to determine whether a bill—authored by Oklahoma Representative Frank Lucas—should be passed to establish the memorial as a national memorial in the National Park Service. The memorial is composed of several parts—empty chairs for the victims; gates to mark the passage of time; an orchard of fruit trees that symbolize the continuing life cycle; and a reflecting pool so that visitors can see the faces of those who are changed forever by the bombing. These elements incorporate the memorial foundation's mission statement to remember those who were killed, those who survived, and those who were changed forever.

Torrey and I will never forget the morning we heard on Voice of America radio while in Berlin, that the Alfred P. Murrah Federal Building in Oklahoma City had been

Hans Butzer, testimony before the Subcommittee on National Parks and Public Lands of the Committee on Resources, U.S. House of Representatives, September 9, 1997.

bombed. Although we were an ocean away, we felt shocked that such a tragedy could occur on American soil. We also believed it to be our duty to make some sort of contribution to the recovery efforts.

The design we are presenting to you is our contribution, and is guided primarily by the introductory paragraph of the Memorial Foundation's Mission Statement:

We come here to remember those who were killed, those who survived and those changed forever.

May all who leave here know the impact of violence.

May this memorial offer comfort, strength, peace, hope and serenity.

The Gates

With these words, the experience of visiting the Oklahoma City Memorial begins. Whether traveling along Harvey Avenue or Robinson Avenue or along Fifth Street, the first sight of the Memorial Complex is of the gates of time. Within the urban fabric, these gates provide a powerful identity for the Memorial Complex and clearly indicate that this portion of Fifth Street has been closed forever. The Eastern gate, inscribed with the time "9:01", together with the Western Gate "9:03" frame the moment and place of explosion "9:02."

The gates also serve as a transition, both physical and psychological, from the busy city streets to a meditative landscape rich with soft edges and sounds.

Beneath the inscription "we come here to remember," one is drawn through the gate's opening into the heart of the moment 9:02 eager to tell its story.

The Chairs

The footprint of the former Alfred P. Murrah Federal Building to the South is covered with soft green grass, sloping up toward the warmth of the sun. The 168 empty chairs are on the grassy slope where the building once stood, reminding us of those who died. While the tragedy has affected the community and nation as a whole, the 168 individual chairs will remind us of the personal loss which resulted on April 19, 1995.

The chairs' presence will ensure that future generations of Americans will always remember these members of our community. The chairs are constructed of a stone seat and back mounted atop a glass block base which is inscribed with a victim's name. By day, the chairs appear to float above their translucent base, just as our memories of loved ones seem to float past at any given moment. By night, the glass bases will be illuminated, representing beacons of hope which will inspire Oklahoma City, its state and the Nation, to rebuild and prepare for a better tomorrow.

The Orchard

The Survivor Tree, witness to the violence of the moment, stands to the north commemorating those who survived. Under its canopy, grassy terraces step down in constrast to the sloping field of 168 chairs beyond. Here, visitors may sit and find inspiration to live their lives more meaningfully, and better appreciate the freedoms they as survivors enjoy.

Rushing forth the city's edges to surround the Survivor Tree, is an orchard of blossoming fruit trees which recognize those who helped. Symbolic in their bearing of fruit, these trees allude to the continuing life cycle of those rescued and their future generations. The harvesting of the fruit in the fall would be the focus of annual celebrations honoring those who helped and those who were rescued.

Nestled in the northwest corner of the orchard is a special place for little helpers—the children. A series of chalkboards set in the ground represents the many letters and drawings the children sent in support, and provides a place for them to continue expressing their thoughts and encouragement.

The Reflecting Pool

A long reflecting pool spans what was once Fifth Street. Gently flowing water soothes the healing wound caused by the fiery blast. The sounds of moving water provide a peaceful background to visitors' thoughts. During the hot summer, the pool will provide cool relief. In winter, its surface may freeze, reflecting the warm glow of the empty chairs.

The Memorial

In 1998 construction began on the memorial that was built on the site of the former federal building. It was dedicated on February 19, 2001, by President George W. Bush. He told the audience that while the time for mourning may pass, the time to remember loved ones never does.

One of the things that we remember of that day in 1995 is the conduct of the leaders of Oklahoma—Oklahoma City and of your State, particularly your Governor [Frank Keating] and his great wife, Cathy. You had just taken office, Frank, and yet, in the aftermath of the awful moment you showed such character and strength. America came to admire that, and the people of Oklahoma will never forget it.

Americans found a lot to admire in Oklahoma during those days. You suffered so much, and you responded with courage. Your loss was great, and your pain was deep, but far greater and deeper was your care for one another. That is what lasts, and that's what brings us back to this place on this day.

Memorials do not take away the pain. They cannot fill the emptiness. But they can make a place in time and tell the value of what was lost. The debris is gone, and the building is no more. Now, this is a place of peace and remembrance and life.

A mother who lost her daughter here will be working in the new museum. She said, "When I come down here to the memorial I've always felt a very good feeling. This is where she was happy, and this is where she was last. The time for mourning may pass, but the time for remembering never does."

Here, we remember one act of malice. The Gates of Time record the very moment of it. Yet, we also remember many acts of human kindness and heroism and love. Some were recorded, some not. But by 9:03 on that morning, a new and hopeful story was already being written. The truth of Oklahoma City is the courage and comfort you found in one another. It began with the rescue; it continues with this memorial; it is recorded in this museum.

Together, you endured. You chose to live out the words of

Saint Paul, "Be not overcome of evil, but overcome evil with good." Because of this spirit, your memorial belongs to all America. People from all over our country come here every day and will always come to look and remember and say a prayer. Oklahoma City will always be one of those places in our national memory where the worst and the best both came to pass. . . .

The evil that destroys and the good that saves are equally real. Both can be taught. Both can be learned. All order in our society begins in the souls of citizens. Character is often shaped or bent early in life. In every family and in every school, we must teach our children to know and choose the good, to teach values that defeat violence, to teach good kids—kids to respect one another, to do unto others, the meaning of love.

Our first response to evil must be justice; yet a part of us is never satisfied by justice alone. We must search for more—for understanding and healing beyond punishment. Faith tells us that all wrongs are righted and all suffering redeemed. But that faith is tested, especially for those of you with empty chairs at home. Hardest of all is the loss of the children, of the lives taken so soon after they were given.

I hope it helps to remember that we are never closer to God than when we grieve. Faith is tested in suffering. And faith is often born in suffering, for that is when we seek the hope we most need; that is when we awaken to the greatest hope there is; that is when we look beyond our lives to the hour when God will wipe away every tear, and death will be swallowed up in victory.

On this Earth, tragedy may come even on a warm spring day, but tragedy can never touch eternity. This is where they were last, but beyond the Gates of Time lie a life eternal and a love everlasting. You in Oklahoma City are victims of tragedy and witnesses to hope. You have overcome evil, and you have suffered with courage. And for that, your Nation is grateful.

God bless.

George W. Bush, remarks at the dedication of the National Memorial Center Museum in Oklahoma City, Oklahoma, February 19, 2001.

Dark reflective stone will line the pool's surface, making it difficult to see the bottom. Water will flow over the edges and disappear into a thin channel running around the perimeter of the pool.

It is here at the water's edge that the areas of the empty chairs, the Survivor Tree and its terraces, the fruit tree orchard meet. And as visitors gaze at their own reflections, they see the faces of those changed forever.

As you can see from our response, this event touched the world. It is our hope that the world will be able to come to the site of this event and gain an understanding of what happened on April 19th. I respectfully urge your support of H.R. 1849, the bill to establish the Oklahoma City National Memorial as a unit of the National Park System and designate the Oklahoma City Memorial Trust.

The Children's Boots

Leonard Pitts Jr.

The site of the Alfred P. Murrah building became a shrine of
sorts following the bombing in 1995. Even before the building was demolished, people began bringing mementos and
leaving them on the chain-link fence that surrounded the site.
Stuffed bears, baby shoes, bouquets, and poems and notes are
the most popular items that are left on the fence.

Miami Herald columnist Leonard Pitts Jr. visited the
memorial in 1999 before it was completed. He describes his
feelings of awe and reverence as he gazed upon the fence dec-
orated with objects that have become holy icons. He writes
that he still felt pain as he thought about the innocent lives
that were lost.

I t is the shoes that stop me.
They are brown and look new, the rubber on the soles
still thick, black and unmarked. They are toddler-size boots,
made for bouncing in sandboxes and climbing on furniture.
They are hanging by their laces from a length of chain link
fence.

I had not planned it this way. Had not made a special effort to be in this particular city during this particular week.
Hadn't even thought about it until I was on the way to catch
the plane for a business trip. That's when I realized:

Oh, God, that's the city where it happened.

Oh, God, it was right around this time of year.

Oh, God, I have to go to the site.

Which is how I have come to be standing here, staring
through chain links into an empty space. Used to be, the Al-

Leonard Pitts Jr., "Child's New Boots Symbolic of Sacred Site in Oklahoma," *Miami Herald*, April 21, 1999. Copyright © 1999 by the *Miami Herald*. Reproduced by permission
of the Copyright Clearance Center, Inc.

fred P. Murrah Federal Building stood on this spot. But it ceased to exist on April 19 of '95. Came down in a concussive explosion that shattered glass for miles around. Took the lives of 168 women and men. And boys and girls. And babies. Lord, babies, too.

A Memorial to the Dead

Now there is only a scar in the earth where the building used to be. And construction machines that sit unused, resting from their labors. A memorial is being built upon this site. One hundred sixty-eight empty chairs. A reflecting pool. A blast-scarred tree representing the survivors. All slowly taking shape behind the fence.

In the meantime, the fence itself is the memorial, festooned with teddy bears and rosary beads, poems and caps, name badges and T-shirts. There is a strand of palm, perhaps from someone's Palm Sunday worship. There is a placard bearing a message from a credit-union worker to his slain colleagues. There are dolls representing the icons of joyous childhood—Snoopy and Minnie Mouse are here. So are Chuckie from "Rugrats" and the Taco Bell dog. There are pictures—somebody's nana, somebody's son, somebody's mom, somebody's baby girl, somebody's dad. Somebody that somebody else loved more deeply than they knew while they had the chance to say. All of them dead now. All of them dead now and gone.

And there are shoes. Hanging heavily from a chain link fence on a windless afternoon.

I am joined by many people. Hundreds, maybe. All filing in soft reverence past the fence, sometimes examining the objects there with a deference ordinarily reserved for religious icons.

For the most part we walk in silence. Indeed, there is a stillness here that seems to swallow sound, to render even footfalls mute. When someone does speak too loudly, it seems an offense against decency itself. Hush, you want to say. This is not a place for talking. This is ground suffering has made sacred.

Besides, even if you talk, what is there to say? What words do justice to the monstrous thing that happened here? What words make it make sense?

Four years later, we've learned so much about the kind of thinking that brought us to this. Learned about a movement of disaffected zealots who take guns into the woods, calling themselves militias and declaring war against the national government. Learned all their crazy theories—black helicopters, U.N. invasion, and God save the white Christian from bowing before the New World Order. We've even met the killer that movement produced, looked into the unfathomable eyes of the crew-cut young man who masterminded this carnage.

Haunting Questions

But somehow I still can't get my mind around it. Still can't answer the questions that haunt me here at the fence, like ghosts.

What cause could have been noble enough, what anger might have been righteous enough, to justify this willful massacre of innocents? To take all these people away?

I am smiled at by somebody's sister, somebody's uncle, somebody's friend. Just glossy images now. Just memories.

And all I get for my questions is more questions. More raw pain.

Silent mourners shuffle past as I pause at a chain link fence touching a rubber sole that has never seen a sandbox. It strikes me that there is nothing quite so empty as a child's new shoe that will never once be worn.

Appendix: The Victims of the Oklahoma City Bombing

Lucio Aleman Jr., 33
Federal Highway Administration safety coordinator. Married, father of two.

Teresa Antoinette Alexander, 33
Nurse's assistant, died while getting a Social Security card for her son. Married, three children.

Richard Arthur Allen, 46
Social Security claims representative. Father of two.

Ted Leon Allen, 48
Economic development specialist for Housing and Urban Development (HUD). Married, five children.

Baylee Almon, 1
One of nineteen children killed—seventeen of which were at the America's Kids day-care center on the second floor of the federal building. A picture of her in a firefighter's arms won the Pulitzer Prize. Her first birthday was the day before the blast.

Diane Elaine Hollingsworth Althouse, 45
HUD program assistant. Mother of two.

Rebecca Anderson, 37
Nurse, killed by falling debris as she was trying to rescue injured victims after the blast. Mother of four children.

Pamela Denise Argo, 36
Data entry specialist for Presbyterian Hospital. She was completing paperwork at the Social Security office concerning the death of her husband a few weeks earlier.

Saundra Gail "Sandy" Avery, 34
Social Security office clerk.

Peter Robert Avillanoza, 56
HUD supervisor. Married, father of five, stepfather of four.

Calvin Battle, 62, and his wife, Peola Battle, 56
Killed while visiting the Social Security office to check on Calvin's disability benefits. Parents of four children.

Danielle Nicole Bell, 15 months
Attended day care at the federal building on Mondays, Wednesdays, and Fridays.

Oleta Christine Biddy, 54
Social Security representative. Married, one son.

Shelly Bland, 25
Asset forfeiture specialist for the Drug Enforcement Administration. Married, one son.

Andrea Y. Blanton, 33
Clerk, Office of Housing for HUD. Married.

Olen Burl Bloomer, 61
U.S. Department of Agriculture budget assistant. Widower, father of one daughter, stepfather to two children.

Lola Renee Bolden, 40
U.S. Army recruiting officer. Two children.

James Everette Boles, 50
Department of Agriculture administrative officer. Married, two children.

Mark Allen Bolte, 28
Federal Highway Administration environmental specialist.

Cassandra Booker, 25
Was applying for Social Security cards for her twin sons. Four children.

Carol L. Bowers, 53
Social Security operations supervisor. Married, one son.

Peachlyn Bradley, 3
Died while accompanying her mother, grandmother, and brother to the Social Security office. The brother, 4-month-old **Gabreon Bruce**, and grandmother, **Cheryl Hammons**, 44, a certified nurse's assistant, also died. Her mother, Daina Bradley, survived, but her leg had to be amputated in order to free her.

Woodrow "Woody" Brady, 41
Self-employed book publisher, was visiting the credit union.

Cynthia Lynn Campbell Brown, 26
Special agent for the U.S. Secret Service. Married for forty days.

Paul Gregory Broxterman, 42
HUD criminal investigator. Married, three children.

Kimberly Ruth Burgess, 29
Federal Employees Credit Union administrative assistant. Married.

David Neil Burkett, 47
Financial analyst at the Office of Southern Plains Native American Programs for HUD.

Donald Earl Burns Sr., 63
Construction analyst at the Office of Southern Plains Native American Programs for HUD. Married, father of three children.

Karen Gist Carr, 32
Advertising assistant for the army recruiting office. Married.

Michael Joe Carrillo, 44
Department of Transportation regional director. Widower, three children.

Rona Linn Chafey, 36
Drug Enforcement Administration special task force worker. Married, mother of two.

Zackary Taylor Chavez, 3
Attending day care at the America's Kids day-care center in the federal building.

Robert Chipman, 51
Financial analyst for the Oklahoma Water Resources Board, located across the street from the federal building. Married, three children.

Kimberly Kay Clark, 39
HUD legal assistant. Engaged to be married.

Peggy Clark, 42
Veterinary medical officer for the U.S. Department of Agriculture. Married, mother of three children.

Antonio Ansara Cooper Jr., 6 months
Attended America's Kids day-care center.

Christopher Cooper II, 2
Had just started attending day care in early April. He was killed with his mother, **Dana LeAnne Cooper**, 24, the director of America's Kids day-care center.

Harley Richard Cottingham, 46
Special agent for the Department of Defense.

Kim Robin Cousins, 33
HUD program support assistant. Married, one son.

Aaron M. Coverdale, 5, and Elijah Coverdale, 2
Brothers killed at the day-care center.

Jaci Rae Coyne, 14 months
Had attended day care at the federal building about five weeks.

Kathy Cregan, 60
Social Security service representative. Widow, mother of three sons.

Richard Leroy Cummins, 55
Department of Agriculture senior investigator. Married, three children.

Stephen Douglas Curry, 44
General Services Administration building mechanical inspector. Married, father of two.

Brenda Faye Daniels, 42
Teacher at day-care center. Engaged to be married, three children.

Benjamin Laranzo Davis, 29
Operations clerk in the U.S. Marine Corps recruiting station. Married, father of one daughter.

Diana Lynn Day, 38
Public housing revitalization specialist for HUD. One son.

Peter Leslie DeMaster, 44
Special agent for the Defense Department. Married, two children.

Castine Deveroux, 49
Program support assistant at HUD. Mother of six.

Sheila R. Gigger Driver, 28
College student visiting the credit union. Married, one daughter, and three months pregnant.

Tylor Eaves, 8 months
Attended day care at America's Kids.

Ashley Megan Eckles, 4
Was killed along with her grandparents **Luther**, 61, and **LaRue Treanor**, 55, in the Social Security office.

Susan Jane Ferrell, 37
Attorney for the legal division of HUD.

Carrol June Fields, 48
Drug Enforcement Administration office assistant. Married, one son.

Katherine Ann Finley, 44
Vice president of operations, Federal Employees Credit Union. Married, one daughter.

Judy Joann Fisher, 45
HUD office clerk. Married, mother of three, stepmother of one daughter.

Linda L. Florence, 43
Secretary at HUD. Married, one son.

Donald Lee Fritzler, 64, and his wife, Mary Anne Fritzler, 57
Killed while checking on Donald's retirement benefits at the Social Security office. Two children.

Tevin D'Aundrae Garrett, 16 months
Attended day care.

Laura Jane Garrison, 61
Hospital admissions clerk, she was picking up retirement forms at the Social Security office. Married, three children.

Jamie Lee Genzer, 32
Federal Employees Credit Union loan officer. Two children.

Margaret Goodson, 54
Claims representative for the Social Security Administration. Married, mother of one daughter, stepmother of three sons.

Kevin Lee Gottshall II, 6 months
Attended America's Kids day care.

Ethel Louise Griffin, 55
Social Security service representative. Married, two sons.

Juretta Colleen Guiles, 59
Underwriter for Single Family Housing, HUD. Married, mother of five children.

Randolph Guzman, 28

Executive officer of the Marine Corps recruiting station. Engaged to be married in March 1996.

Kayla Marie Haddock-Titsworth, 3

Attended day care.

Ronald Vernon Harding, 55

Social Security service representative. Father of three children.

Thomas Lynn Hawthorne Sr., 52

Local tire company worker and pension and insurance representative for a local union, he was killed while picking up paperwork for a union member at the Social Security office. Married, three children.

Doris Adele Higginbottom, 44

Purchasing agent for the Department of Agriculture. Married, two stepchildren.

Anita Hightower, 27

A secretary, she was killed while at her desk in a building across the street from the Alfred P. Murrah Federal Building.

Thompson Eugene Hodges Jr., 54

HUD supervisor. Married, four children.

Peggy Louise Jenkins Holland, 37

Computer specialist for the U.S. Army recruiting center. Married, two children.

Linda Coleen Housley, 53

Loan officer at the Federal Employees Credit Union. Married, mother of three, stepmother of two.

George Michael Howard, 45
HUD development director. Married.

Wanda Lee Howell, 34
Day-care attendant. Married, two children.

Robin Ann Huff, 37
Loan officer at the Federal Employees Credit Union. Married, two stepchildren.

Anna Jean Hurlburt, 67, and her husband, Charles Hurlburt, 73
Anna Jean was a semiretired nurse, and Charles was a retired professor and director of dental radiology at Oklahoma University. Both were killed while checking on retirement benefits at the Social Security office. Four children.

Paul Douglas Ice, 42
U.S. Customs Service special agent. Two daughters.

Christi Yolanda Jenkins, 32
Federal Employees Credit Union teller. Married, mother of four.

Norma Jean Johnson, 62
Executive secretary at the Department of Defense. Married, four children.

Raymond Johnson, 59
Volunteer administrative assistant at the Social Security office. Married, seven children.

Larry James Jones, 46
Computer programmer with the Federal Highway Administration. Married, three children.

Alvin Junior Justes, 54
Retired government employee, killed while at the Federal Employees Credit Union.

Blake Ryan Kennedy, 18 months
Attended America's Kids day care in the federal building.

Carole Sue Khalil, 50
Export document clerk at the U.S. Department of Agriculture. One daughter.

Valerie Jo Koelsch, 33
Marketing director at the Federal Employees Credit Union.

Carolyn Ann Kreymborg, 57
Automation clerk at HUD. Married, two children.

Teresa Lea Lauderdale, 41
Secretary at HUD. Widow, mother of two sons.

Catherine Mary Leinen, 47
Collection officer at Federal Employees Credit Union. Two children.

Carrie Ann Lenz, 26
Legal technician at the Drug Enforcement Administration. Married, one son.

Donald R. Leonard, 50
Special agent for the Secret Service. Married, three sons.

Lakesha Levy, 21
An airman first class in the U.S. Air Force, died while picking up her Social Security card. Married, one son.

Dominique R. London, 2 years, 11 months
Attended day care.

Rheta Ione Bender Long, 60
Program clerk at the Department of Agriculture. Two children.

Michael Lee Loudenslager, 48
General Services Administration planner-estimator. Rescued a coworker before he died. Married, two children.

Aurelia Donna Luster, 43, and her husband, Robert Lee Luster, 45
Were killed while visiting the Social Security office. Six children.

Mickey Bryant Maroney, 50
Secret Service special agent. Married, two children, one stepson.

James Kenneth Martin, 34
Civil engineer for the Federal Highway Administration.

Gilbert Xavier Martinez, 35
Pastor, died while visiting the Social Security office. Married, father of five, including a son who was ten days old.

Tresia Jo Mathes-Worton, 28
Federal Employees Credit Union teller.

James Anthony McCarthy, 53
Director, Office of Housing, HUD. He had been in his new job for three weeks at the time of the bombing. Married, three children.

Kenneth Glenn McCullough, 36
Special agent for the Drug Enforcement Administration. Married, two children.

Betsy Janice McGonnell, 47
HUD clerk. Two children.

Linda Gail Griffin McKinney, 47
Office manager at the Secret Service office. Married, one son, one stepdaughter.

Cartney (Koch) McRaven, 19
An airman first class in the U.S. Air Force, she was at the Social Security office to report the change of her last name. She had been married four days before the blast.

Claude Arthur Medearis, 41
Senior special agent for the U.S. Customs office. Married, two children.

Claudette Meek, 43
Vice president of financial services, Federal Employees Credit Union. Married, two children.

Frankie Ann Merrell, 23
Federal Employees Union teller. Married, one daughter.

Derwin Wade Miller, 27
Social Security claims representative.

Eula Leigh Mitchell, 64
Was at the Social Security office filling out retirement forms with her husband, who survived. Married, one son, three stepchildren.

John Clayton Moss III, 50
Chief of advertising for the U.S. Army recruiting office.

Patricia Ann "Trish" Nix, 47
Financial analyst, Office of Public Housing, HUD. Married, two children.

Jerry Lee Parker, 45
Engineer for the Federal Highway Administration. Married, father of three children.

Jill Diane Randolph, 27
Certified public accountant for the Federal Employees Credit Union.

Michelle Ann Reeder, 33
Administrative assistant at the Federal Highway Administration. Married.

Terry Smith Rees, 41
Director, Program Operations Division, Office of Public Housing, HUD. Married.

Mary Leasure Rentie, 39
Public revitalization specialist, Office of Public Housing, HUD. Married, two daughters.

Antonio C. Reyes, 55
Equal opportunity specialist for HUD. Married, father of two children.

Kathy Ridley, 24
A student, was killed while visiting an office building across the street from the federal building. Mother of two children.

Trudy Rigney, 31
Geographic information systems intern for the Oklahoma Water Resources Board located across the street from the federal building. One son.

Claudine Ritter, 48
Collection officer at the Federal Employees Credit Union. Two children.

Christine Nicole Rosas, 22
Receptionist at the Federal Employees Credit Union. Married, one son.

Sonja Lynn Sanders, 27
Chief teller of operations at the Federal Employees Credit Union. Married, two children.

Lanny Lee David Scroggins, 46
Staff accountant for the Office of Southern Plains Native American Program, HUD. Married, father of two sons.

Kathy Lynn Seidl, 39
Investigative assistant at the Secret Service office. Married, mother of one son, stepmother of one son.

Leora Lee Sells, 57
Secretary in the legal division at HUD. Married.

Karan Denise Shepherd, 27
Loan officer at the Federal Employees Credit Union. Married, two daughters.

Chase Dalton Smith, 3
Attended day care.

Colton Smith, 2
Attended day care.

Victoria Lee Sohn, 36
A master sergeant with the U.S. Army recruiting office. Married, five children.

John Thomas Stewart, 51
Director, Program Management Division, Office of Public Housing, HUD. Married, father of three.

Dolores Marie Stratton, 51

Military personnel clerk at the U.S. Army recruiting office. Married.

Emilio Tapla, 50

Died checking on disability benefits at the Social Security office. Widow, six children.

Victoria Jeanette Texter, 37

VISA program manager, Federal Employees Credit Union. Married, one son.

Charlotte Thomas, 43

Appointment clerk at the Social Security office. Married, mother of three sons.

Michael George Thompson, 47

Field representative for the Social Security office. Married, four children.

Virginia Mae Thompson, 56

Worker at the Federal Employees Credit Union. Three children.

Rick Lee Tomlin, 46

Special agent, division program specialist for the Department of Transportation. Married, two sons.

LaRue Ann Treanor, 55, and her husband, Luther Hartman Treanor, 61

Killed at Social Security office while checking on Luther's retirement benefits. Parents of four children.

Larry Laverne Turner, 42

Special agent for the Department of Defense. Married, father of one son and one stepson.

Jules Alfonso Valdez, 51
Program manager, Office of Southern Plains Native American Program, HUD. Married, one daughter.

John Karl Van Ess III, 67
Review appraiser for Office of Housing, HUD. Married, four sons.

Johnny Allen Wade, 42
Engineer for the Federal Highway Administration. Married, father of two children.

David Jack Walker, 54
Environmental officer for HUD. Married, three daughters.

Robert Nolan Walker Jr., 52
Social Security claims representative. Married, one son, four stepchildren.

Wanda Lee Watkins, 49
Clerk in the U.S. Army recruiting office.

Michael D. Weaver, 45
Attorney, legal division, HUD. Married, two sons.

Julie Marie Welch, 23
Social Security claims representative.

Robert Glen Westberry, 57
Special agent in charge at the Department of Defense. Married, father of three children.

Alan Gerald Whicher, 40
Assistant special agent, U.S. Secret Service. Married, two children.

Jo Ann Whittenberg, 35
Program support assistant at HUD.

Frances Ann Williams, 48
Secretary, Community Planning and Development Division at HUD. Mother of two.

Scott Dwain Williams, 24
Seafood salesman, was killed while making a delivery at the federal building. Married, one daughter.

William Stephen Williams, 42
Operations supervisor at the Social Security office. Married, three daughters.

Clarence Eugene Wilson, 49
Area counsel, Legal Division, HUD. Married, one son.

Ronota Ann Woodbridge, 31
Pavement materials engineer for the Federal Highway Administration. Married.

Sharon Louise Wood-Chesnut, 47
Social Security claims representative. One daughter.

John Albert Youngblood, 52
Special agent, Office of Motor Carriers, Federal Highway Administration. Married, father of five.

Chronology

1992

August 21–22: Federal law enforcement agents surround the home of Randy Weaver in Ruby Ridge, Idaho, to arrest him on weapons charges. During a gun battle that lasts two days, Weaver's fourteen-year-old son and wife are killed as well as a U.S. marshal. A criminal investigation into the shooting leads to dismissal of the weapons charges against Weaver due to entrapment, and the U.S. Justice Department is ordered to pay him $3.1 million in compensation for the deaths of his family members.

1993

February 28: Agents from the Bureau of Alcohol, Tobacco, and Firearms (ATF) surround the compound of the Branch Davidian sect in Waco, Texas, to arrest its leader, David Koresh, on weapons charges and to serve a search warrant. Someone fires a shot, and during the following gun battle, six Davidians and four ATF agents are killed. The FBI takes charge and begins a fifty-one-day siege of the compound.

April 19: The FBI brings in a tank to knock down the Branch Davidian compound's walls. Fires break out in several places in the compound; Koresh and about eighty of his followers, including twenty-one children, are killed in the fires.

November: Congress passes the Brady Law, which mandates a five-day waiting period for all handgun purchases.

1994

September 13: Timothy McVeigh starts planning to blow up a federal building.

September 30: McVeigh and Terry Nichols buy forty fifty-pound bags of fertilizer from a farming co-op in McPherson, Kansas, using the alias Mike Havens.

October 1: McVeigh and Nichols steal explosives from a military storage magazine in Marion, Kansas, and then drive the stolen explosives to Kingman, Arizona, where they store them in a storage unit.

October 18: McVeigh and Nichols buy a second ton of fertilizer in McPherson, Kansas.

October 21: McVeigh visits a motorcycle racetrack in Texas and buys racing fuel worth $2,775 to use in the bomb.

November 5: McVeigh and Nichols rob a gun and coin dealer in Arkansas of firearms, ammunition, coins, and gold and silver bars. They store the stolen property in a storage unit rented under the name Ted Parker in Council Grove, Kansas.

December 16: McVeigh drives Michael Fortier past the Alfred P. Murrah Federal Building in Oklahoma City and tells him the building is his target.

1995

January–February: McVeigh and Nichols sell the stolen firearms from the Arkansas robbery to finance the bombing. Fortier is given a portion of the proceeds.

April 14: McVeigh buys a 1977 Mercury Marquis at a service station in Junction City, Kansas. He subsequently checks in to the Dreamland Motel in Junction City.

April 16: McVeigh drives his car to Oklahoma City and leaves it parked on a street near the federal building. Nichols drives him back to Kansas.

April 17: Using the alias Robert Kling, McVeigh rents a Ryder truck from Elliott's Body Shop in Junction City. He and Nichols then proceed to transform the rental truck into a truck bomb using the fertilizer and racing fuel they had purchased several months earlier.

April 19: McVeigh parks the Ryder truck on the north side of the Murrah federal building. The bomb explodes at 9:02 A.M.; the entire north side of the building disappears in the blast. The explosion kills 168 people, including 19 children, and injures several hundred people. McVeigh is arrested on weapons charges at approximately 10:30 A.M. after a routine traffic stop near Perry, Oklahoma, about seventy miles north of Oklahoma City. The FBI discovers the rear axle of the Ryder truck used in the bombing and traces it through its vehicle identification number to Elliott's Body Shop in Junction City. Agents get a description of Robert Kling and an unknown accomplice who rented the truck. The address used on the rental agreement leads to a farm in Decker, Michigan, belonging to James Nichols, brother of Terry Nichols.

April 20: Sketches of John Doe Number 1 and John Doe Number 2, the suspects who rented the Ryder truck, are released. Employees at the Dreamland Motel recognize John Doe Number 1 as Timothy McVeigh, who stayed at the motel registered under his own name.

April 21: The FBI discovers that McVeigh is being held in jail in Perry on weapons charges. He is charged with the bombing and is taken to a federal prison in El Reno, Oklahoma. Terry Nichols surrenders to police in Herington, Kansas.

April 23: A memorial service for victims of the explosion is held in Oklahoma City. President Bill Clinton, the Reverend Billy Graham, Attorney General Janet Reno, and more than ten thousand others attend.

May 4: The bodies of Christine Rosas and Virginia Thompson still remain in the destroyed federal building when the search for survivors is finally called off.

May 8: A memorial service is held for the two remaining bodies in the rubble.

May 10: Terry Nichols is charged in the bombing.

May 23: The remains of the Murrah building are imploded.

August 10: Timothy McVeigh and Terry Nichols are indicted by a federal grand jury on three counts of conspiring to use a weapon of mass destruction to kill people and destroy federal property and eight counts of killing federal workers while in the performance of their duties. Michael Fortier pleads guilty to a minor firearms charge as part of a plea bargain. He is to be sentenced after McVeigh's trial.

1996
February 20: A U.S. District Court judge orders that McVeigh's trial be moved to Denver due to intense media coverage of the bombing in Oklahoma.

1997
March 31: Jury selection begins for McVeigh's trial.

June 2: The jury convicts McVeigh on all counts.

June 13: The jury imposes the death sentence on McVeigh.

September 29: Jury selection begins for Nichols's trial.

December 23: The jury convicts Nichols of conspiracy to use a weapon of mass destruction and involuntary manslaughter for the deaths of eight federal agents. He is found not guilty of using a weapon of mass destruction and destruction by explosive.

1998
January 7: The jury is deadlocked on the sentence for Nichols. The judge orders the lawyers to file briefs on the punishment phase for Nichols.

May 27: Michael Fortier—who knew of the bombing plot and failed to warn authorities but testified against McVeigh—is sentenced to twelve years in prison on weapons charges.

June 4: Nichols is sentenced to life in prison.

2000
April 19: The Oklahoma City National Memorial is dedicated on the former site of the Alfred P. Murrah Federal Building.

December 28: McVeigh drops all appeals of his execution.

2001
January 16: McVeigh's execution date is set for May 16.

May 10: The U.S. Justice Department acknowledges that it found more than three thousand pages of evidence that should have been provided to McVeigh's defense attorneys.

May 11: U.S. attorney general John Ashcroft orders that McVeigh's execution be delayed for thirty days to give lawyers an opportunity to review the new evidence.

Early June: McVeigh instructs his lawyers to reopen his appeal of his execution. After a judge denies a stay of execution, McVeigh orders his lawyers to once again drop his appeal.

June 11: McVeigh is executed by lethal injection at the federal prison in Terre Haute, Indiana.

2003
May 5: A preliminary hearing begins in Oklahoma City to determine whether there is enough evidence to try Terry Nichols on Oklahoma state murder charges for the deaths of 160 victims of the bombing.

May 13: A preliminary hearing in Oklahoma City determines there is enough evidence to try Terry Nichols on Oklahoma state murder charges for the deaths of 160 victims of the bombing. A trial date of March 1, 2004, is set.

For Further Research

Books

Marsha Brock Bishop and David P. Polk, eds., *And the Angels Wept: From the Pulpits of Oklahoma City After the Bombing.* St. Louis, MO: Chalice, 1995.

Mark S. Hamm, *Apocalypse in Oklahoma: Waco and Ruby Ridge Revenged.* Boston: Northeastern University Press, 1997.

Jon Hansen, *Oklahoma Rescue.* New York: Ballantine, 1995.

David Hoffman, *The Oklahoma City Bombing and the Politics of Terror.* Venice, CA: Feral House, 1998.

Clive Irving, ed., *In Their Name: Dedicated to the Brave and the Innocent, Oklahoma City, April 1995.* New York: Random House, 1995.

Stephen Jones and Peter Israel, *Others Unknown: The Oklahoma City Bombing Case and Conspiracy.* New York: Public Affairs, 1998.

Marsha Kight, *Forever Changed: Remembering Oklahoma City, April 19, 1995.* Amherst, NY: Prometheus, 1998.

Edward T. Linenthal, *The Unfinished Bombing: Oklahoma City in American Memory.* New York: Oxford University Press, 2001.

Andrew MacDonald, *The Turner Diaries.* 2nd ed. Washington, DC: National Alliance, 1980.

Lou Michel and Dan Herbeck, *American Terrorist: Timothy McVeigh and the Oklahoma City Bombing.* New York: Regan, 2001.

Kerry Noble, *Tabernacle of Hate: Why They Bombed Oklahoma City.* Prescott, Ontario, Canada: Voyageur, 1998.

Oklahoma Bombing Investigation Committee, *Final Report on the Bombing of the Alfred P. Murrah Federal Build-*

ing, April 19, 1995. Oklahoma City: Oklahoma Bombing Investigation Committee, 2001.

Lana Padilla with Ron Delpit, *By Blood Betrayed: My Life with Terry Nichols and Timothy McVeigh.* New York: HarperPaperbacks, 1995.

Jim Ross and Paul Myers, eds., *We Will Never Forget: Eyewitness Accounts of the Bombing of the Oklahoma City Federal Building.* Austin, TX: Eakin, 1996.

Richard A. Serrano, *One of Ours: Timothy McVeigh and the Oklahoma City Bombing.* New York: Norton, 1998.

Kenneth S. Stern, *A Force upon the Plain: The American Militia Movement and the Politics of Hate.* New York: Simon & Schuster, 1996.

Brandon M. Stickney, *All-American Monster: The Unauthorized Biography of Timothy McVeigh.* Amherst, NY: Prometheus, 1996.

Kathleen Treanor with Candy Chand, *Ashley's Garden: One Family's Journey, from Grief to Spiritual Restoration, in the Aftermath of the Oklahoma City Bombing.* Kansas City, MO: Andrews McMeel, 2002.

Periodicals

Paul Baumann, "An Editorial Dissent," *Commonweal*, May 19, 1995.

Arlene Blanchard, "One of the Lucky Ones," *Essence*, April 2000.

Phil Blanchard, "The Prison Letters of Timothy McVeigh," *Esquire*, May 2001.

Commonweal, "To Kill or Not to Kill," May 19, 1995.

Tracy Daugherty, "After Murrah: An Essay on Public and Private Pain," *Southwest Review*, Fall 1998.

Brian Duffy, "The End of Innocence," *U.S. News & World Report*, May 1, 1995.

Bruce Frankel, Bill Hewitt, and Pam Lambert, "Aftermath: Looking Back, Some of Those Whose Lives Were Torn

Apart by the Bombing Tell How Time Has Dealt with Their Wounds," *People*, April 24, 2000.

Nancy Gibbs, "The Blood of Innocents: In the Bomb's Aftermath, Tales of Horror and Heroism," *Time*, May 1, 1995.

Lauren Janis, "At the Execution," *Columbia Journalism Review*, July 2001.

Steven Lewis, "Shattered Innocence," *Parenting*, August 1995.

Flynn McRoberts and Andrew Murr, "'I Thought I Was Going to Die,'" *Newsweek*, June 18, 2001.

New Yorker, "Back from the Void," May 15, 1995.

Rosie O'Donnell, "When I Was a Kid, I Depended on the Death Penalty," *Rosie*, July 2002.

Mark Peyser, "Survivor: 'All I Saw Were Bright Lights,'" *Newsweek*, June 5, 1995.

Johanna Schneller, "They Watched Him Die," *Rosie*, July 2002.

Cintra Scott, "After the Bomb," *Seventeen*, May 1996.

Stan Statham, "Dead Man Watching," *Vital Speeches of the Day*, July 1, 2001.

Heather Taylor and Tish Durkin, "Aftershocks: What I Saw, What I Did, and Why I Tried to Kill Myself," *Mademoiselle*, April 1996.

Jacob Weisberg, "Playing with Fire," *New York*, May 8, 1995.

Websites

ABC News, http://more.abcnews.go.com/sections/us/oklahoma/bombing.html. ABC News includes comprehensive coverage of the bombing, including a list of the victims killed, brief biographies of the key people involved in the bombing and the trial, and a complete transcript of Timothy McVeigh's trial.

CNN, www.cnn.com/US/OKC. The CNN website includes information on the bombing, the case against Timothy McVeigh, the reporters who covered the bombing, transcripts of the Terry Nichols trial as well as links to other sites about the bombing.

Oklahoma City Bombing Investigation, www.okcbombing. org. The Oklahoma City Bombing Investigation Committee spent four years interviewing eyewitnesses and researching the bombing of the Alfred P. Murrah Federal Building. It published *Final Report on the Bombing of the Alfred P. Murrah Federal Building, April 19, 1995*, in which it concludes that the federal government had prior knowledge of the bombing and did nothing to prevent it. It also maintains that McVeigh had help planning and executing the bombing beyond that provided by Terry Nichols.

Oklahoma City National Memorial, www.oklahomacity nationalmemorial.org. This official website of the Oklahoma City National Memorial includes complete information about the memorial and the Memorial Institute for the Prevention of Terrorism.

U.S. Department of Justice, www.usdoj.gov/oig/special/ oklahoma/fullpdf.htm. Following the discovery of more than three thousand pages of evidence that had not been released to Timothy McVeigh's lawyers prior to his trial for the bombing, the Office of the Inspector General (OIG) ordered an investigation of the FBI's handling of the evidence. This website includes the OIG report and its conclusions that the FBI did not deliberately withhold evidence.

Index